A Portrait of Heaven's Love

A Portrait of Heaven's Love

Kirk Gilchrist

Scripture quotations are from the New King James version of the Bible.

Hebron Press
2120 E. 11 Mile Rd.
Royal Oak, Mich. 48067

ISBN 0-9647871-6-4

Book Cover designed by Identity Graphics - 1-810-543-9550

For Worldwide Distribution
Printed in the U.S.A.

For More Information call 1-800-527-8329 or write to the address listed above.

ACKNOWLEDGEMENTS

I would like to thank the Lord, first and foremost for His blessing upon the life of my family. I can honestly say that we have done nothing to deserve what we have received. We could never repay Him for what He has given!

I would like to thank my wife for her heart of giving throughout the years. Without her selfless heart, I realize that I would not have been given the opportunity to receive any of the truths that are mentioned in this book. Therefore, any blessing received for this book will be her reward and not mine. May God bless her as she has blessed and given to me. I love you Carolyn!

I would also like to thank all who gave in the editing of this book. Grammar has never been my strength, and there have been multiplied hours given by many friends. This book of love has already been bathed in love due to their sacrifice and giving. Thank you very much!

Lastly, I would like to thank a close friend for his wonderful artwork. Bill Kleist and I have been friends for a long time, and I have always appreciated his talent. I never considered, however, that he would design a cover for a book that I had written. His talent is obvious and God given. Thanks Bill, for your friendship and artwork.

PREFACE

The life of John presents one of the most dramatic expressions of God's love man has ever known. I can honestly say that no other message has penetrated my heart quite like the message of the first epistle of John. John was known to be the Apostle of love, and it seems very fitting that he was also chosen to reveal ***the God of love***.

Before I began the process of writing this book, I needed the assurance that it was God's will. As I sought the Lord, He blessed me with His (seal of) approval on my endeavor. There have been multiplied hours of careful editing and tedious changes, as there is for any book. Yet, throughout the entire project, the Spirit of the Lord has been there to give His blessing and grace. I believe with certainty that it is God's will, and I trust that I may present it as God's book. I would hope that others may meet the Lord as much in reading this book as I did while writing it.

Thousands of writers dedicate their lives to writing books and publishing them. When I questioned whether this book would be worth the time and energy, God quickly refuted my doubts with a simple thought. If one person's life is touched (or affected for eternity), all my time and energy will seem very insignificant. In comparison to God's great sacrifice of love for humanity, the sacrifices we make are as a speck of sand on a seashore. How humbling it is when God reveals to us the price He paid and the love He has for His people.

There were times during this project that I searched my heart for any impure motives, such as self-promotion or man's approval. I must honestly say that God has checked my heart many times during the different stages of writing this book. God has constantly reminded me that I can do nothing without Him. Many times I have attempted to accomplish things by my own efforts, only to see disastrous results. My only motive for this book is that each reader may fall deeper in love with the Lord and experience a deeper and closer relationship with their Father. I believe this was John's purpose for his first epistle, and it is the reason I have chosen to write this short expository. My hope is that on the completion of this book, each reader will be inspired and drawn to seek the Lord as never before. May each one experience a greater fervency in their walk and relationship with their God. I have no higher hopes for this book, and it will be judged by no other merits.

INTRODUCTION

John, the Beloved of the Lord, and His First Epistle

In a sunlit room, the congregation sat in quiet anticipation. They knew that soon their feeble old leader would rise and share with them God's own heart. This man had seen much of the Lord; he had been in prison for his faith and had often endured harsh and extreme tortures at the hands of his enemies. The old man, though, was not filled with bitterness or broken by hatred, as many would have been; but instead there was vibrancy and joy radiating from him.

Within the church one of the young pastors now stood and asked for wisdom from the old leader, "Brother, what is the Lord saying to us today?" With quiet and graceful determination, the old man forced his legs to respond and slowly lifted himself from the stone bench where he had been sitting. "The word for today is to love the Lord and to love your neighbor as yourself." On the following day this group of faithful Christians again came together and asked of their leader, "Brother, what is the Lord saying to us today?" just as before, this feeble old man gracefully stood and declared, "The word for today is to love the Lord and to love your neighbor as yourself."

On the following day, the group was filled with excitement knowing that their trusted leader had received something fresh from the throne of God, "What is it that he will say to us today?" they all wondered. Finally, one of the young pastors stood; this was to be a special day that would be remembered for all of eternity by both man and angel. "Brother, what is the Lord saying to us today?" he eagerly asked. Once again, this feeble old man would willfully stand and declare, "The word for today is the word that all those who are close to the throne will hear: the word for today and every day is to love the Lord your God and to love your neighbor as yourself."

The name of this leader was John, the beloved of the Lord.

Though we might read the preceding paragraphs as a fictitious scene in the mind of the author, I believe we will see through the pages of this book that the message of this story, if indeed it is fiction, was much deeper in truth in the life of John than we could have possibly envisioned here. John was a man who knew God, a man who knew the ways of God, much like Moses, "He made known his ways unto Moses, his acts unto the children of Israel" (Psalm 103:7). John was also a man of intense love; he loved his closest friend with the same appealing love as he loved his enemy. John's worst enemies were those within the same church, who had heard the same message he had heard. The epistles of John were written to those in the household of faith who rise up against their fellow believers. He had a deep desire for the Body of Christ to be a forgiving and loving people, much like the young carpenter he had walked with so many years before. Surely John must have been near the Lord's side many times and witnessed Christ's profound love and endless compassion for His people. As we study this first epistle may we open our hearts as never before and receive this heart that John had seen, heard, and testified of. May we lay aside our differences, learn from the old leader, and rise from our stone benches declaring to one another, "Though we might not agree, you are my brother by the blood of Christ, and I love you!" Let us study together the words of this love letter and learn the heart of our Shepherd as He expresses Himself through a man called John.

Chapter 1

A Man Called John

The first thought in understanding any book lies within the author. Who is John? What made John so special? Why did God choose this man as the deliverer of this message? John was a unique individual; his life is diverse and full of seeming contradiction. Perhaps there is not a more powerful example of how God can change a life in all of Scripture. The thought that this insignificant fisherman could become a writer of the anointed words from Heaven is one of the greatest miracles Heaven has ever produced, and his study provides great hope that God can also take our lives and make us into men and women of the Kingdom.

Who Is John?

If we could go back into history and observe the Last Supper from a distance, what would we see? We would stand in amazement if we could for a moment watch with understanding the twelve men walking with the Lord. We understand that one of them is to be the betrayer - his name is Judas. What would we see of the other eleven? We know some were men of power and some were former tax collectors, but perhaps the greatest truth we could understand is what they all were collectively. They were all men of doubt. They were all men who still argued with Jesus about the Cross up to the day of His death. They were men of little understanding. Yet, in the wisdom of Heaven, they were all diamonds. Diamonds in the rough? Yes, but diamonds!

The diamond is the hardest of all known natural materials. It is an interesting stone in the fact that fewer than 20 percent of the diamonds mined each year are suitable for use as gems. Finished stones are graded according to quality and then marketed. Various classification systems are used: color, clarity (freedom from flaws and inclusions), cut, and carat weight. The market value is based on the grading of each individual diamond. The stones are then finished in various kinds of cuts. The best proportioned ones are those that throw back the most light.

How God has chosen to reveal Himself through nature has always been astounding. Great elements of truth can be gleaned as we study the process that a stone is taken through to become a diamond. We will see that the disciples also experienced this process of refinement. They were, in the eyes of natural men, stones that should have been rejected. Yet God, in His infinite wisdom, knew that John, as well as the other disciples, were simply unpolished stones. They were men of error and unfounded thought. They were men who loved their own way and had great plans for themselves. Yet, they were also men in whom God delighted to reveal once again that He is a life-changing God. For John would be a pure diamond that would shed much light, a diamond of true quality. What can we see in the upbringing of John that would help us understand how God was polishing this individual stone?

JOHN, AND HIS YOUTH

John was raised in the home of Zebedee and Salome. Zebedee, as his name implies, was "a gift" to this young man. He was a fisherman by trade. From what we can read in the Gospel accounts, he would also teach his sons to walk in these same steps. The fishing business was a hard business. It required long hours and was very physical in nature. So, John was taught from his youth to be a hard worker which most likely gave him some advantages. He would be physically strong, accustomed to danger, able to endure hardship at sea, and he would most likely be mature for his age because of his responsibilities. The Gospels further reveal that John most likely came from a wealthy home. We read in Mark 1:20 that there were hired servants in the boat with Zebedee and his sons.

Though Zebedee had servants, it seems he still knew the importance of teaching his children to work. He knew, believed, and taught that the wisdom of Proverbs was a necessity for his children. He would take it as a personal challenge to impart to them what was important in life and prepare them for the days ahead. What if his business would fail? What if his children would depart to another way of life? What if he would die? What would help his children in any of these circumstances? Zebedee's diligent work ethic would carry over from his business to his home, making him a faithful parent in raising his children to follow God's ways.

The Lord also gives us a beautiful picture of the call of God, desiring His children from all walks of life to be overcomers. For example, Jesus taught that it is hard for a rich man to enter the Kingdom of heaven, yet we also read that with God all things are possible. God would use John and his brother James to reveal His goodness. He shows Himself to be a God who can take the rich and give them a heart and a call for the kingdom. What a wonderful picture of God's mercy.

Salome, John's mother was another blessing to him. Her name means "the peaceful one," and if we could read between the lines, we would probably see a picture of a peaceful, godly wife.

Zebedee, John, and James after a hard day of working would longingly begin their journey home. The Gospels do not reveal to us how far they lived from their fishing village, but the trip home must have been filled with quiet anticipation and thoughts of home. The word home can have many different meanings to many different men. For some it is a place of struggle, a place of hardship. For others, it is only an empty place filled with quiet and a lack of true life. For others, perhaps, it is a place filled with rambunctious behavior, and the lack of activity is not a problem here, *too* much activity is this home's problem. For Zebedee and his boys, we would most likely see something far different than these other homes. If Salome was truly full of peace, as her name implies, we could make some assumptions as to how she obtained that peace. It doesn't seem too presumptuous to say that she must have loved to spend time in the presence of her God. Peace comes when we're in constant communion with our Creator. Her days must have been filled with singing and prayer as she went about her household duties. Salome, "the peaceful one," most likely filled her days with worship, and as she worshipped she must have received a deeper hunger for God. The Bible reveals that she went to Jesus and asked a request on behalf of her two sons, that they might be those with honor in the Kingdom of Heaven (Matthew 20:20-21), this reveals she must have had a deep spiritual desire and a vision for her children. The sons and husband of Salome would walk into a home filled with rest, filled with the aroma of a freshly prepared meal, but more importantly a home that was filled with the presence of the Lord.

The imprint of both his parents emerges clearly throughout John's life. We can see in him Zebedee, the strong fisherman, walking with Jesus village by village, mile after mile, ministering and trudging forward with the Lord. Yet, in quiet moments and in the beautiful picture given during the Last Supper, we can see shades of Salome, the peaceful one, as John rested his head upon the heart of Jesus. The Lord used both his parents to begin the work of polishing this diamond in the rough. Others would follow, but the work started with his wonderful parents, Zebedee and Salome.

His Discipleship under John the Baptist

Further preparing him for his life's work was John the Baptist. Though we cannot conclusively prove that John was a disciple of John the Baptist, there are some scriptural reasons to assume this. In John 1:35 we read, "Again, the next day, John (the Baptist) stood with two of his disciples. And looking at Jesus as He walked, he said, "Behold the Lamb of God." One of the disciples here with John the Baptist was Andrew, Simon Peter's brother, as we can see in verse 40 of this same chapter. The other disciple is believed by most scholars to be John, the beloved. The reason for this is that John never mentions his own name in his Gospel, though he seemingly always mentions the names of others (see John 19:34 and John 21:24). John was an eye witness of what he wrote about, so the only way he possibly could have known about this statement by John the Baptist is if he was there.

In the Baptist's statement, "Behold! The Lamb of God who takes away the sin of the world!" (John 1:29), John was forever changed. For the particular way a person comes into the Kingdom of God can affect them all their lives. John for instance, was introduced to Jesus as the "Lamb of God" and will refer to the "Lamb" 28 times in the book of Revelation. It became his message and theme.

A number of years ago, I was also instructed about the Lord in a similar manner. In fact, the deepest word I have *ever* received came through my four year old son on that day. As most fathers often do, I was sitting in our recliner reading something that seemed very important to me at the time (like the morning paper, a book, etc..) when Benjamin ran up and said, "Hey, Dad, can I tell you something?" "Can't you see I'm reading?" I replied sternly. After a few moments, Benjamin again ran up, "Hey, Dad, can I tell you something?" Again I responded in a similar manner,

"Benjamin, I told you I'm reading, now go back in your room and play." After what seemed like a few moments to an adult, but probably an eternity to Benjamin, he returned (the monster from the black lagoon), "Hey, Dad, can I tell you something?" The third time I was extremely annoyed, and considered Benjamin out of line, and very, *very* sternly I replied, "Benjamin, do you need to be disciplined? I told you to go back into your room. Now what do you want?" The words that he would speak would be the most cutting words that God has ever spoken to me. "Daddy, do you know that Jesus is a Lamb?" With that, I could only reply, "Yes, Benjamin, I know that Jesus is a lamb, and I know, Ben, that I am not one." As I thought of the love, mercy and selflessness of the Lamb, I replied, "Please, Ben, don't be like your Dad; be like the Lord who is the Lamb." From that day forward, I have set my face to be more like the Lamb who would and does lay down His life for His family. The Lamb that John met that day changed his life. The Lamb I met that day still changes lives. Being like the Lamb became the message of John... it was what John lived to be.

Interestingly, the name John comes from the Hebrew name Jonah, meaning "a dove, or the Lord is gracious." This was to typify John's life. In the Gospels, we read that John and his brother James were given a much different name by the Lord. They were called "Boanerges," the "Sons of Thunder" (Mark 3:17). Yet, in all of our accounts of John, we never again see him with this title. On the other hand, Simon who was named Peter, often referred to his new name. Why? In his heart, I believe John cried out, "Let me be John - the dove, the gracious one." The most important thing in John's life was not to be a son of thunder, one full of zeal, full of intensity, full of power, yet lacking in mercy and patience. The most important thing was to be like the One he had met so many years before, the Lamb of God. Are we, as Christians, following after the One whom we are named for, or do we forget that Jesus is introduced to us first and for all time as "the Lamb of God who takes away the sin of the world"? John learned this lesson early in his life under the teaching of John the Baptist, and he would later teach this same truth, not as theory, but as life. What would he learn from his Master, the Lord Jesus Christ? The epistle of First John will give us a clear answer. To understand this letter, let us first consider the timing of the book that John has given us.

"And John cried out, LET ME BE JOHN, the dove, the gracious one."

The Timing of His Writing

John's first epistle is believed to have been written sometime previous to A.D. 95. The Roman emperor Domitian began to persecute the Church extensively during that year, and John does not mention this in his epistles. Domitian was the last Roman emperor of the Flavian Dynasty. Although he had not held any important post during the regimes of his father, Vespasian, and his older brother, Titus; he was allowed his claim to the throne after the death of Titus in A.D. 81. He is one of history's most disturbing cases. He was the first emperor to demand worship as a god while he was alive. Many emperors were worshipped after their death, but he was the first while still living. His reign was known as "the reign of terror" which he initiated in A.D. 89. Provoked by a rebellion in Germany, Domitian began to attack senators and officials he mistrusted and began to suppress even the mildest forms of dissent. However, these attacks backfired since they inspired many conspiracies - which is just what Domitian had feared. He managed to survive most of the attempts on his life, but on September 18, A.D. 96, he was murdered by assassins who had been paid by his wife.

It is in this historical setting that John wrote his first epistle. During a time of hatred, John would write of love. During a time of a crazed emperor, John would write of a leader without flaw. During a time of killing, John would write of One who had been crucified for all. History provided a wonderful background for this letter, and John would use this background masterfully. Now let us go on to the first epistle of John to better understand God's message through a man called John.

Chapter 2

WALKING IN THE LIGHT

FIRST JOHN 1

The Theme for this Book: 1 John 1:1-4

John reveals the theme for this epistle during his introduction.

> *That which was from the beginning, which we have heard, which we have seen with our eyes, which we have looked upon, and our hands have handled, concerning the Word of life; the life was manifested, and we have seen, and bear witness, and declare to you that eternal life which was with the Father and was manifested to us; that which we have seen and heard we declare to you, that you also may have fellowship with us; and truly our fellowship is with the Father and with His Son Jesus Christ. And these things we write to you that your joy may be full.*

John's purpose for writing this epistle was to reveal Christ. We could correctly assume that as the basis for every book of the Old and New Testament, which would lead us to ask, What makes this book so different? The answer is really quite simple. John is not writing about a Lord he has only heard about; he is writing about the Lord he has **personally** heard and **personally** seen. John was able to say Christ is the risen Lord because he had experienced it. He had seen and heard the risen Savior. He will unveil for us the Gospel of John. Furthermore, he states that he writes to us that our joy may be full. When the Christian walk becomes reality, not fiction or theory, we will then and only then experience what real Christian joy is. It is not a feeling or a sensation; it is a relationship.

This then will be our theme throughout the first epistle of John: "That which we have **seen** and **heard** we declare to you... that your joy may be full."

Walking in the Light: 1 John 1:5-7

This is the message which we have heard from Him and declare to you, that God is light and in Him is no darkness at all. If we say that we have fellowship with Him, and walk in darkness, we lie and do not practice the truth. But if we walk in the light as He is in the light, we have fellowship with one another, and the blood of Jesus Christ His Son cleanses us from all sin.

It is not enough to reveal the written word of God, people must see *the* Word of God in our lives. John could declare God is light because he knew it by experience. He had seen his Master reveal this truth in his hearing and in his sight. Remember, this is John's theme, revealing the Lord whom he had seen and heard. Consider the following examples from the Gospel of John.

> *Then Jesus spoke to them again, saying, "I am the light of the world. He who follows Me shall not walk in darkness, but have the light of life." (John 8:12)*

> *Now as Jesus passed by, He saw a man who was blind from birth. And His disciples asked Him, saying, "Rabbi, who sinned, this man or his parents, that he was born blind?" Jesus answered, "Neither this man nor his parents sinned, but that the works of God should be revealed in him. "I must work the works of Him who sent Me while it is day; the night is coming when no one can work. "As long as I am in the world, I am the light of the world." When He had said these things, He spat on the ground and made clay with the saliva; and He anointed the eyes of the blind man with the clay. And He said to him, "Go, wash in the pool of Siloam" (which is translated, Sent). So he went and washed, and came back seeing. Therefore the neighbors and those who previously had seen that he was blind said, "Is not this he who sat and begged? Some said, "This is he." Others said, "He is like him." He said, "I am he." Therefore they said to him, "How were your eyes opened? "He answered and said, "A Man called Jesus made clay and anointed my eyes and said to me, 'Go to the pool of Siloam and wash.' So I went and washed, and I received sight." (John 9:1-11)*

John writes that Jesus Christ is light and that this light can cleanse us from all sin. How could he write this with such boldness? How can we know that he was correct in his writings? By what authority did John speak? The answer is *experience*. This was not theory to him; he had been there when the Light of the World had opened the eyes of the blind. He knew that God was light. He had heard it with his ears, and he had seen it with his eyes.

Oh, that we might by experience declare that He is our Savior. Many Christians can explain the theories of the Kingdom, but John was one who shared what he *knew!* He was a man who was willing to be taught. When the Light of the World declared Himself to John, it was no surprise that John so readily believed the words of his Master. He had learned from his youth to be a teachable. We must remember that Zebedee had **taught** John the ways of a fisherman; from his youth he was made to listen and obey.

It is a sad truth that so many parents do not teach their children to learn. Disobedience is excused and rationalized away. There seems to be an overwhelming attitude or approach to life that is present in the world today. It begins in children, and because it is allowed to remain in children, it therefore works its way into the adult world. We so often see that every person does what is right in his or her own eyes. As Christians, many would disagree with this observation. However, when was the last time that someone presented a case in contradiction to your preconceived ideas and you sat down and really considered it? How readily do you admit that you may be wrong?

Let me share a nugget of truth with you. The word *disciple* has a definition; we cannot possibly be a disciple unless this definition is working in our lives. The word *disciple* means "to be a learner." Unless we are learners, we cannot be disciples. John, as well as all of the disciples (except Judas, who should be a powerful example to us!) were learners. How would you like to have been called those "of little faith"? This was not stated to the disciples just once but five times in the Gospels. Jesus was rebuking, correcting, and instructing the disciples right up to His death. And they became men of God, men capable of leading others, because they themselves knew what it was like to be led.

Today there are many teachers in the Kingdom. There are those who declare that they are called to be the teacher of the teachers. This is a noble thought, yet there is one thought much more noble, much more honorable. There is a thought that can only be understood by those who qualify to be a disciple. John knew it and is declaring it throughout his epistle. We do not want to be the teachers; we want to be the learner of the learners. With this heart, we, like John, can declare experientially what we have learned. We can declare what we have seen and heard. Jesus, who is the Light of the World, has come to reveal light to all those who are willing to be His disciples. This light will penetrate and repel all darkness, if we will simply admit our need for light and for understanding. Are you a learner? Are you like John? May his love for the Lord inspire you to follow his example and become a disciple in and of the light!

Are You the Learner of the Learners?

Forgiveness of Sin - First John 1:8-10

If we say that we have no sin, we deceive ourselves, and the truth is not in us. If we confess our sins, He is faithful and just to forgive us our sins and to cleanse us from all unrighteousness. If we say that we have not sinned, we make Him a liar, and His word is not in us.

Here we see John beginning to deal with the subject of sin and the forgiveness of sin. It is interesting to note that John brings out this truth in the beginning of his letter and throughout the entire book. John understands, as we must also understand, that there is no possibility of moving on in God until this subject of sin is dealt with. Jesus has told us in John 3:3 that "unless a man is born again, he cannot see the kingdom of God." However, this letter is written to Christians. Why would John deal with a subject that has already been taken care of? Every person, in order to be a Christian, has already accepted Jesus as Savior and Lord (meaning the master, the controller) of his or her life.

John emphasizes this point because he knew and understood two important facts. First, it is hard for Christians to forgive themselves; and second, it is hard for Christians to forgive the world. Yet, John was able to counter balance these truths with confidence, as he writes to us that *GOD WILL FORGIVE.* He knew this from experience. One particular story, among many from his Gospel will illustrate this.

John 8:1-11 But Jesus went to the Mount of Olives. Now early in the morning He came again into the temple, and all the people came to Him; and He sat down and taught them. Then the scribes and Pharisees brought to Him a woman caught in adultery. And when they had set her in the midst, they said to Him, "Teacher, this woman was caught in adultery, in the very act. Now Moses, in the law, commanded us that such should be stoned. But what do You say? This they said, testing Him, that they might have something of which to accuse Him. But Jesus stooped down and wrote on the ground with His finger, as though He did not hear. So when they continued asking Him, He raised Himself up and said to them, He who is without sin among you, let him throw a stone at her first. And again He stooped down and wrote on the ground. Then those who heard it, being convicted by their conscience, went out one by one, beginning with the oldest even to the last. And Jesus was left alone, and the woman standing in the midst. When Jesus had raised Himself up and saw no one but the woman, He said to her, Woman, where are those accusers of yours? Has no one condemned you? She said, "No one, Lord." And Jesus said to her, "Neither do I condemn you; go and sin no more."

What a powerful example of how far Christ will go to forgive sin! John had heard and seen this incident. Maybe he was confused thinking, How can this be? How could He speak like that to this woman? Doesn't He know what she has done?

A number of years ago, I heard a story told about this incident that I believe to be accurate. What was Jesus writing in the sand? The Bible reveals to us that they had caught this woman in the act of adultery. Her accusers were right. She was guilty of sin, but could any of her accusers declare to be sinless themselves? As they began pressing Jesus for an answer, let us put His words in today's English, "If any of you live a perfect life, then judge her." He then does a very curious thing - He begins to write again in the sand. The disciples must have been thinking, What is He doing? How could He be so blasé at this crucial moment? What was He writing in the sand? We then read that these accusers began to walk away one by one. Why? Just a few moments before, they were filled with wrath. I believe they left because Jesus was confronting them with their own sins. He would look into the eyes of each man, with those eyes that must have confronted every sin, and would begin to write that man's sin in the sand. To the man who hated others, He would write, "You shall not kill." To the man full of lust, He would write, "You shall not covet your neighbor's wife." To the man who was unfaithful in giving, He would write, "You shall not steal." No wonder they would leave one by one! How could they, who were also guilty of sin, condemn this woman? Jesus then turned to the woman and revealed the deepest desire of the heart of God, the reason He had come: "Neither do I condemn you, go and sin no more."

What a wonderful lesson John had seen and heard that day. It is no wonder that in the first epistle of John he had such clarity. John knew that he served a forgiving God. We must be careful about thinking that our perception is God's perspective. We do not see as He sees. This woman looked guilty and was guilty. Yet God, in His wisdom and understanding, saw redemption and forgiveness. May we truly understand, as John must have that day, that our thoughts are not His thoughts nor our ways His ways.

To what extent does God reveal how He forgives? Consider the most powerful examples of the men of God in the Bible. We would have to name at the top of our list Abraham, Moses, David, Peter, and Paul. These are only a few examples of God's forgiveness. They were all men who loved God; yet they were all men who failed God. Abraham was a liar, yet became the "father of faith." Moses was a murderer and became the "mighty deliverer." David was an adulterer and a murderer, yet in the book of Acts is called "a man after God's own heart." Peter was a denier of the faith and became the one who would speak to thousands about his faith. Paul was also a murderer (of the brethren) and became the chiefest of all apostles. Why? Because our God is not only a forgiving God, but a life-changing God who has revealed this to all generations through the lives of these men. Their lives are an example of how far God will and can go in the forgiveness of sin in a Christian's life. This does not excuse sin, but it does elevate the love and forgiveness of God toward His people.

> *But God commendeth his love toward us, in that, while we were yet sinners, Christ died for us.* ***Much more then, being now justified by his blood, we shall be saved from wrath through him.*** *For if, when we were enemies, we were reconciled to God by the death of his Son,* ***much more, being reconciled, we shall be saved by his life.*** *(Romans 5:8-10)*

Chapter 3

LOVING, OBEYING AND ABIDING

FIRST JOHN 2

Christ our Advocate: 1 John 2:1-2

My little children, these things I write to you, so that you may not sin. And if anyone sins, we have an Advocate with the Father, Jesus Christ the righteous. And He Himself is the propitiation for our sins, and not for ours only but also for the whole world.

This chapter would seemingly start out the same as the previous section of Scripture that we have studied. Yet the difference lies in the fact that the Lord will forgive an individual such as the adulterous woman, and now we see that forgiveness being applied to the world.

John, in these verses, also writes from his firsthand experience with Jesus.

The next day John saw Jesus coming toward him, and said, "Behold! The Lamb of God who takes away the sin of the world!" (John 1:29)

"For God so loved the world that He gave His only begotten Son, that whoever believes in Him should not perish but have everlasting life. For God did not send His Son into the world to condemn the world, but that the world through Him might be saved. (John 3:16,17)

Then Jesus said, "Father, forgive them, for they do not know what they do." And they divided His garments and cast lots. (Luke 23:34)

These verses are very specific. God is not only interested in the individual, He is interested in the world. John, who was at the foot of the cross during the crucifixion of Christ, most likely heard directly what Luke had written, and we could safely assume that he must have heard the other sayings upon the cross as well. These sayings can give us insight into what John is writing in his epistle about God's love and commitment to the world. As we look at the seven sayings upon the cross, we want to consider them with this thought in mind, How is God revealing His love to the world through them? There are many wonderful books written on the deep theological truth that we can receive from these sayings; however, that is not our emphasis. We are looking at what John saw. What did John hear that would cause him to write with such passion about God's love? May these words ring in our ears and cause us to live with a wonderful hope for those that are without hope and in need of the experience of the cross in their lives.

Seven Sayings upon the Cross

Before we study or examine these seven sayings, we must remember that the life of Christ is not a story; it is a way of life. This was not an allegorical look at the life of a fictional character. This was a real man, with real pain, in real agony giving His life for the world. Anybody's last words are highly esteemed. When a person is about to be executed, the question is always asked, "Do you have any last words?" These words are always very carefully recorded and always very highly considered. It is in these words that truth (perhaps in the lives of some men for the first time) is most often spoken. There is nothing to gain, and nothing to lose with these last words.

In this picture of Jesus hanging upon the cross, we can see tremendous agony. His beard had been ripped from His face. He had been beaten numerous times. The crown of thorns had been placed upon His head. The nails driven through His hands and His feet. The Bible tells us that His body had become marred more than any other man. The picture of a Savior beautified is not the true picture of the cross. He was in agony, and it was from this agony that He spoke perhaps some of the most important and convincing words to the unbeliever that could be spoken. If there was to be malice, certainly it would have come out now. If there was any inconsistency, surely now we would have seen it. But it is here, upon the cross, that Jesus pours out what He truly is. It is here in these seven sayings upon the cross that we are gripped (again) with His deep love and concern for every person who has ever been born into this world. It is here that every argument is diffused and the heart of Jesus is seen in reality.

1. "Father, forgive them, for they do not know what they do." (Luke 23:34)

John could write about the forgiveness of the Savior because he had seen and heard it personally. In the midst of Jesus' agony, we find forgiveness being spoken of. There was no outcry against His accusers, no outcry against those who had bruised and beaten Him. In the scene of the cross, there is only forgiveness. What a wonderful Savior, though we reject and we wound Him, He speaks of forgiveness. His true heart is revealed. If He would utter those words then, how much more now? The sin problem was solved on that day and is forever solved. Jesus cannot, nor ever will, remove those words. John had seen and heard from the cross about the wonderful forgiveness of his God.

2. "Assuredly, I say to you, today you will be with Me in Paradise." (Luke 23:43)

What was Jesus saying to the world? What was He saying to each individual? In *His* darkest hour He was revealing that grace is still available to all. In *our* darkest hour, grace is available! His last companion on earth was a thief. But as He had revealed with the woman with the issue of blood, with blind Bartimaeus, and with so many others, He always longs for those in need of healing. Corrie ten Boom said it so well, "There is no pit so deep that Christ is not deeper still." In His deepest moment of agony, we see a true revelation of what He is. He is a God who is willing to give grace and mercy to those who are needy. The only prerequisite to need fulfilled, is need acknowledged. In the mind and heart of John, he must have considered that if this thief (who had mocked Jesus only a few moments earlier) could find forgiveness, then surely there is no one to whom Christ would withhold forgiveness.

> The only prerequisite to need fulfilled, is need acknowledged.

3. *"Behold, your son!....Behold your mother!"* (John 19:26,27)

This is a wonderful illustration of how individually the Lord will reveal His love for the world. Here we can understand what the Lord feels about the widow and the fatherless. James writes to us in his epistle that "*pure and undefiled religion before God and the Father is this: to visit orphans and widows in their trouble.*" On the cross, Jesus is found ministering to this group which is so close to His heart. He is helping us understand that there is no group too insignificant for the love that only the cross could reveal.

Consider for a moment the heart of an earthly father. If I were to allow my kids to be in the care of another for a time, and upon my return I found out that they had not been fed or clothed, I would be outraged! I would deal harshly with the perpetrators. This depicts the heart of God the Father. If we reject the child or the orphan we literally reject the Father. It is an honor to be able to give to this group of people. Why? Because they are the children of the Heavenly Father. Jesus was revealing to us His deep love for those who are so often forgotten by the world. As the Psalmist wrote of God's heart, *God stands in the congregation of the mighty; He judges among the gods. How long will you judge unjustly, And show partiality to the wicked? Defend the poor and fatherless; Do justice to the afflicted and needy. Deliver the poor and needy; Free them from the hand of the wicked* (Psalms 82:1-4).

4. *"My God, My God, why have You forsaken Me?"* (Matthew 27:46)

Why was He rejected? For *you,* that's why! Meditate on the power of that statement for a few moments. Why was Jesus forsaken, why was He beaten, why was He bruised, why the agony, why the pain? For ***you!*** He was forsaken so that ***you*** might have access to the Father. He was forsaken so that ***you*** may be purged. He hung upon the cross, rejected for ***you.*** It is no wonder that John wrote with such conviction. He had seen the forsaken Son cry out, "Why have You forsaken Me?" and he answered the question, for ***you!***

5. *"I thirst."* (John 19:28)

The One who had never thirsted, for the first time, was spiritually thirsty. There are some who would say that Jesus was never spiritually thirsty. However, the Bible tells us that He became sin for us. When Jesus hung upon the cross, He was guilty for the sin of all humankind. That is the reason He never defended Himself with Pilate, Herod, or the religious leaders. He *had become sin* for us; He *was* guilty. Even the Father had to accept the guilt of His Son and acknowledge Him worthy of the punishment of the cross. The greatest sacrifice and revelation of the love of the Son was witnessed in these words on the cross. The Son who had always experienced the pleasure of relationship with His Father, had now given up that relationship to become the sin offering for humanity, and the Father had given up His relationship with His Son. What a sacrifice! There was always only one reason for this, "*For God so loved the world that He gave His only begotten Son, that whoever believes in Him should not perish but have everlasting life.*" John had heard these words and had now seen them manifested by the fact that Jesus gave up all so that we might know that He loves and forgives. Again, I want you to see the importance - "He became sin for us, for you." This should inspire us to want to love Him with everything that is within us.

6. *"It is finished!"* (John 19:30)

These are perhaps the most triumphant words in the whole Bible - "It is finished!" The enemy had lost! What other Scriptures can we read to gain further understanding to this statement?

Colossians 2:13-15 And you, being dead in your sins and the uncircumcision of your flesh, hath He quickened together with Him, having forgiven you all trespasses; Blotting out the handwriting of ordinances that was against us, which was contrary to us, and took it out of the way, nailing it to His cross; And having spoiled principalities and powers, He made a show of them openly, triumphing over them in it.

1 Corinthians 1:17-18 For Christ did not send me to baptize, but to preach the gospel, not with wisdom of words, lest the cross of Christ should be made of no effect. For the message of the cross is foolishness to those who are perishing, but to us who are being saved it is the power of God.

Galatians 6:14 But God forbid that I should boast except in the cross of our Lord Jesus Christ, by whom the world has been crucified to me, and I to the world.

Colossians 1:20 And, having made peace through the blood of His cross, by Him to reconcile all things unto himself; by Him, I say, whether they be things in earth, or things in heaven.

Romans 8:37-39 Yet in all these things we are more than conquerors through Him who loved us. For I am persuaded that neither death nor life, nor angels nor principalities nor powers, nor things present nor things to come, nor height nor depth, nor any other created thing, shall be able to separate us from the love of God which is in Christ Jesus our Lord.

The cross, and only the cross will defeat every enemy and every influence that is contrary to God. Yet, in our lives, we so often wonder why we don't experience the power of the cross. Where is this relationship working in us? Why are we dry? Why don't we have victory? Why don't we see miracles? Where is the power of the blood? As John stood gazing at the scene of the cross, perhaps he wondered and he contemplated these same questions. What was the answer? What had John seen and heard? The answer is within the last statement upon the cross.

7. *"Father, into Your hands I commend My spirit."* (Luke 23:46)

Jesus was first and foremost, beginning to end, a man of relationship. When it seemed to gain Him nothing and the "seventy" were leaving Him, He continued to give His life to the Father. The cross will always look foolish to those on the outside. The average Israelite must have thought that it was foolish for this young 33 year old man to give His life in such a way. Yet, it is through the cross experience that death brings forth life. What is the key to the cross? "*Into Your hands I commend My spirit.*" It is when we totally yield our spirit, as Jesus did, that we will receive this blessing of the cross.

Do you want the power of the cross? Then commend your spirit to the Lord. He will eradicate sin from your life and cause the nature of the Lamb to birthed within you. He will always choose what is best for your life. He will choose your ministry, whether it be to many or few according to His choice and His knowledge. John's understanding was enlightened as he stood gazing upon the cross. He knew of the wonderful depth of the forgiveness of God. He had seen and heard that the forgiveness of Christ touches every individual and, in turn, the world.

Obedience to His Commandments

First John 2:3-6

And hereby we do know that we know him, if we keep his commandments. He that saith, I know him, and keepeth not his commandments, is a liar, and the truth is not in him. But whoso keepeth his word, in him verily is the love of God perfected: hereby know we that we are in him. He that saith he abideth in him ought himself also so to walk, even as he walked.

One fresh crisp autumn morning I found myself sitting in the northern woods of Michigan. Squirrels playfully scurried past the place I was sitting and would squeal at their sudden awareness of my presence. Suddenly, off to my right I noticed the movement of a larger animal. I was on a bow hunting trip and was hunting for whitetail deer. I slowly positioned myself for a shot at one of the two large doe that were now moving in my direction. I had hoped that they would come down a trail that would place them in perfect position only 15 yards from where I was waiting. As they moved one small step after another, I realized that the shot I had anticipated was exactly the shot I would be given. As the largest of the two deer stood in that exact spot, I slowly pulled my bow string back and released the arrow. I knew the shot would be as perfect as the location of the deer. The deer ran at the sound of the release of the string, yet I thought there must be an arrow in the side of the animal. Upon inspection of the area, I was stunned to find my arrow in the ground near where the deer had stood. What had I done wrong? How could I have missed the deer? I pondered this question as I waited for another chance. Maybe I had misjudged the distance. Maybe I had not released properly. I knew that I had not practiced like I should have, but I had hunted plenty of times to know how to shoot and how to maneuver around this very wily animal. Suddenly the two doe returned, following the same trail (or runway for those of you who are deer hunters). I was amazed; they must not have known where the sound came from. As if it were ordained from heaven, these two doe were walking the same path and walking to the exact same spot. Again, I pulled my bow and again I released my arrow. Only to once again, find my arrow in the same area, covered with the under hair of the deer that I had merely grazed. I was flabbergasted: What had I done? Shortly after I returned to my position, I spotted movement from the opposite direction that the doe had come from. As I looked, I was shocked to see a large buck now coming in my direction. It was walking down the same path that the doe had walked down. I now knew why this had all happened. The Lord wanted to bless me with a large buck; He didn't want me to only shoot a doe. He, my heavenly Father, wanted to bless me with a buck. Unbelievably, the buck stopped in the exact spot where the doe had stopped. I knew everything about this shot. I pulled and released my arrow and watched the buck run away. I knew this animal would soon be dead. It was only a matter of following the blood trail and finding the deer. As I walked to the spot, I quickly spotted my arrow. I knew that it would give me the necessary information as to where I had hit the deer. On inspection of the arrow, I was amazed to find that once again I had only grazed the lower portion of the deer. There was no blood and no deer. I even made a large scan of the area to be sure. There was no doubt, I had missed the same shot three times. What had gone wrong? I sat down and began to ask the Lord for the reason. God spoke something that day that has changed my perspective on life. "Without preparation, we cannot hit the mark for our lives." I knew what the Lord was saying: Without the proper amount of practice, I could not expect to hit the spot that I had aimed. What a spiritual truth God was revealing to me! It is only possible for us to fulfill God's purpose for our lives as we allow Him to have complete control of our lives. This is what John will begin to write to us about. If we are truly friends of God, we will be those that walk in obedience to His commands, allowing Him to prepare our lives according to His perfect will.

As John continues to declare the things he has seen and heard, he is also deepening his message. He began by declaring to us the forgiveness of God and is now revealing to us the commitment that comes with that forgiveness. We are not forgiven only to remain or return to our old life-style. The Bible tells us that Jesus has come to give us life abundantly. *This* is the life that John had experienced and seen. He knew by walking with and observing the Lord that He was full of life and that if we would walk as He walked, we could also experience this joy for living that he had seen and heard.

"This is My commandment, that you love one another as I have loved you. Greater love has no one than this, than to lay down one's life for his friends. You are My friends if you do whatever I command you. No longer do I call you servants, for a servant does not know what his master is doing; but I have called you friends, for all things that I heard from My Father I have made known to you. You did not choose Me, but I chose you and appointed you that you should go and bear fruit, and that your fruit should remain, that whatever you ask the Father in My name He may give you. (John 15:12-16)

It is important to understand that Jesus is talking about a call that is much more personal than the call given to Adam. When we consider the Garden of Eden, we often conclude that it was the most wonderful place. It was a place filled with the presence of God. It was a place filled with peace and joy and happiness. Yet, the call of the present-day Christian is a call much greater than Adam's. Adam was **created** in the likeness of God. It required no choice on his part and no decision to follow after God's presence. It was always there. However, in the life of a Christian, we are not created in the likeness of God - much differently, we are born into the sin of Adam. Yet, God in His mercy had devised a plan. It would not please the heart of the Father to force mankind into a relationship with Him. He desires a love relationship. He desires those who have loved His presence and been **conformed** into His image. **Conformed** rather than **created**. This is a love relationship. After Adam's fall, man's choice to follow and serve the Creator would be solely based on a decision dictated by love. This is what John had seen and heard. Obedience to His commands will determine and prove whether we are friends or servants.

It is interesting to note what the actual meaning of this word "command" found in John, chapter 15 actually means. It does not connote the thought of a robot or someone that is forced to carry out God's will for their lives. It actually comes from two Greek words that mean "custom through intimacy." It reveals the thought of being so like your master that you actually think, act and speak like him. God is not looking for little robots who follow His every command. He is looking for intimate friends who spend so much time with Him that they are actually like Him.

In the world, and unfortunately often times in the church as well, there is a major emphasis placed on money. Have you ever wondered what God's concept about money is. As we are considering this thought of friendship and being like the Lord, let's look at a natural example in our lives that reveals what we are speaking about. The Bible tells us that God loves a cheerful giver. Have you ever wondered why? We can read in the book of Revelation that the streets of heaven are paved with gold. This gives us a Scriptural revelation about God's concept of gold. His gold is equal to our concrete or gravel covered streets. God does not place an important emphasis in His Kingdom on money or gold. So then, why does God love a cheerful giver? Because it is a revelation of what He is. God desires to have fellowship with those that are like Him. It is not the amount of money that a person possesses, and in turn gives, that pleases God; it is the attitude of the heart. God, Himself, loves to give. He is constantly pouring out blessings upon His children. Henceforth, the reason that God loves cheerful giving is because those that give with that kind of heart are those that have become like the Lord in that area of their lives. These are people that have entered into true friendship and intimacy with their Master.

The Bible tells us that Jesus will reveal Himself to His friends. The reason for this is quite simple: He is longing and looking (as any friend would), for friends who serve Him because they love Him, not because they are obliged to. A friend is told all things; if we want to be those who understand the secrets of God, we must be obedient to His commands. There is an interesting verse found in the book of Luke that says, "Well done, good servant; because you were faithful in a very little, have authority over ten cities (19:17)." One of the most important doctrinal statements is found in this little verse: A friend is faithful and can be trusted with greater truth. A friend is willing to be corrected and can be instructed in a deeper measure. Why? Because a true friend can be given the smallest task and be expected, because you are friends, to care deeply about the completion of that task. A true friend can hear the harshest and the gentlest word from a friend and continue to care deeply about that relationship. Why? Because they are friends.

Many Christians desire to live their lives as servants of God. However, the level of commitment and sacrifice involved in true servant-hood is sadly lacking in the Church today. We know that the word "servant" comes from the thought of being a slave. Can you imagine with me what would happen to many "servants" in the Kingdom of Heaven, if they were natural servants. Imagine if the master of the house would come home and say, "Servant, please bring me my slippers." Only to hear in reply, "Master, I do not have a witness in my spirit that I should get your slippers." Or maybe the master would say, "Servant, I am hungry, would you please bring me some grapes?" Only to have the servant return to the room with a plate full of bananas, "Master, I know what's best for you, and you will eat these bananas instead." We know what would happen to this unfaithful servant. He would lose his job and maybe his head. How can it be that in the Church the Master of the Universe speaks and we so often do not reply, or we reply with our own motives or self-interest? How willing are we to obey our Master? This is the truest test of our maturity in Christ. When the Lord speaks, are we quick to reply and run after the Bridegroom? When the sweet voice of our Beloved calls for us at 3:00 in the morning, are we so in love with His presence that we long to serve our Master whenever He might call?

If you cannot be trusted by God with that which is little, you have not entered into true friendship. John had seen Jesus correct, chasten, rebuke, and admonish those He loved. John had seen the difference between Judas who refused to be corrected, and Peter who when corrected was able to receive. Are you listening to the Master? Are you a doer of the word? A friend is a hearer *and* a doer.

"Without Preparation We cannot Hit the Mark for our Lives"

The Message of Love (Part 1)

1 John 2:7-11

"Brethren, I write no new commandment to you, but an old commandment which you have had from the beginning. The old commandment is the word which you heard from the beginning. Again, a new commandment I write to you, which thing is true in Him and in you, because the darkness is passing away, and the true light is already shining. He who says he is in the light, and hates his brother, is in darkness until now. He who loves his brother abides in the light, and there is no cause for stumbling in him. But he who hates his brother is in darkness and walks in darkness, and does not know where he is going, because the darkness has blinded his eyes."

What was John referring to when he said that we have had the commandment since the beginning? If we were to travel back in time to the beginning of life as we know it, to the book of beginnings, Genesis, we would see and hear God looking down upon a destitute and forgotten earth and saying, "Let there be light." What greater expression of love could the world ever ask for? God, the eternal Father, knew what humanity would do to His Son and how they would often reject and ridicule Him. He knew that as He lovingly chose to give life to this world, they would someday choose to take life from His own dear Son.

God's purpose for the ten trials of Israel is greatly misunderstood by many in the Body of Christ today. It is one of the greatest revelations of the love of God that is recorded for us in the Scripture. It is believed that after the tenth trial the children of Israel crossed the line of no return. Some say they came to the place where God cut them off. That because of the error in their lives, their murmuring, and their complaining, God finally had enough of their problems and removed them. This is inconsistent with the reason that Jesus came and His very life. This is inconsistent with the heart of God and the revelation of Himself throughout the whole of Scripture. Let's look at the ten trials and see, if perhaps, God was trying to reveal something completely different, something wonderful, something divine.

The ten trials seem to be the thread that is woven throughout the journey of Israel from Egypt and into the land of Canaan (the land of promise). We know that the journey began with great hope and wonderful victory. The Israelites, through their leader Moses, had witnessed the miraculous intervention of God in their deliverance. They must have begun their journey rejoicing and believing that life would be one blessing after another. I believe the heart of God longed for an opportunity to reveal His character, His life and specifically His names to the children of Israel. Let's consider these ten trials and see how God would seek to reveal one aspect of His character or one of His names in each specific trial and how by the end of the trials, God had to remove the old generation before they could enter into the land of promise.

The Ten Trials

1. Opposition from the World

El Shaddai = God Almighty

The first trial began shortly after the Israelites left Egypt. This would surely have been the greatest challenge they had faced so far. The enemy, seeing that he had lost ground, began a major attack against them. Although, with the attack, God made a way of escape, we can see three things at the Red Sea. It was meant to bring hope to the Israelites as they saw the destruction of Egypt. It was also used as an act of judgment against Pharoah. More importantly, it was God revealing Himself to His people. The Israelites had a wonderful opportunity. They could understand and experience God as their God, El Shaddai. He was the Almighty God who could part the Red Sea and destroy every enemy. God's heart must have rejoiced in showing Himself to His people. How sad that His people then, as they do today, rejected this name and quickly turned against their leader.

2. Bitter Water - Murmuring

Jehovah Shalom = God of Peace

The Israelites next trial in the journey led them to Marah. Having gone for three days without water, they came to an oasis in the midst of the wilderness. What relief they must have felt to know their thirst would be satisfied.

Finally, they could quench the thirst of their children. Finally, they could water their camels and bathe their children. (Only to find out upon closer inspection that the waters of Marah was bitter.) Here Israel, after seeing some of the most incredible miracles ever shown to mankind, failed the test. They had forgotten God's power and missed the message that God was longing to reveal to them. Jehovah Shalom, the God of Peace, was walking in the midst of this experience trying to reveal to them, that in the midst of the darkest trials, the love and peace of God (Jehovah Shalom) is there to be found.

In obedience to the Lord, Moses threw a tree into the waters, and the waters turned sweet. How often in our lives are we in the same situation and miss this opportunity to meet God and know Him in a deeper measure. (Rather than trusting our God in time of need,) we also rise up and murmur. God, though, is saying that the key in this story, as well as in every story, is the "tree." It is the Cross that will bring life. It is the Cross that will bring us the power needed to overcome the bitter experiences of life. It is only in death, as we lay this body to rest that we can understand the sweet peace that only Jehovah Shalom can bring. Israel had an opportunity on earth to learn this wonderful aspect of God's divine nature. May we not fail this test but fall in love with God Almighty, Jehovah Shalom.

3. No Bread - Hunger

Jehovah Jireh = God our Provider

How the heart of God rejoiced! Here was another chance, another place that God could reveal Himself to His people. They were hungry; they needed something to eat. Surely, God their God could provide their every need. They had seen this at the Red Sea, and they had seen this in the land of Egypt. Now, here was a name that they would understand. He would reveal Himself as Jehovah Jireh, the Lord their provider. We know the Lord provided both quail and manna for His people. He was showing them what a wonderful opportunity they had to understand the character and nature of God in a deeper way. In every trial that He leads us through, God's purpose is to reveal Himself to us. We too, as Christians, are called to know God by His individualistic names and reveal Him to others. It is sad as we continue to read this story of the ten trials that we see Israel did not understand this, and in fact, failed to remember this character of God in their next opportunity to meet God.

There was a time for my wife and I that God did a wonderful work revealing Himself to us as Jehovah Jireh. As a young couple, we found ourselves struggling financially. I was working very long hours but still never seemed to have quite enough to make ends completely meet. At this time, we received the wonderful news that my wife and I were expecting a baby. It was a time of great joy, and the anticipation was wonderful. I suppose as a man I didn't realize that there were many things we needed for the baby. What a surprise I had in store! One day my wife informed me that we needed five basic items: a crib, a mattress for the crib, a car seat, a changing table, and a high chair. Then I began to fret, how are we going to buy these items? We didn't have any extra money. Finally, in desperation, I turned to the Lord in prayer and asked Him to provide these items. We never told anyone, and at this point we were trusting in the provision of the Lord. A few days later my brother called, "Hey Kirk, I have a crib that I am no longer using, would you like it?" "Yes, I'll take that crib," I replied with great joy. A few days after that my mother called, "Kirk, I know that your brother gave you a crib and your father and I would like to give you a mattress for the crib, would you like it?" "Hmmm," I teasingly pondered, "Yes we would love to have that mattress," I replied. A few days later my father-in-law showed up at the front door, "Hey Carolyn, I was at Sears and they had these car seats on sale, so I bought you one." "Oh, thank you! We can definitely use that car seat," she replied. A few days later along came her father again, "Carolyn, I was at Sears and they had these changing tables on sale, do you need one?" "Yes, I think that is still on our list!" she answered knowingly and joyfully. God provided the last item as I was working on a woman's car in the church. She came out of her house with a highchair in hand, "Kirk, I have this highchair that we are not using, do you think that you and Carolyn could use it for the new baby?" I responded with pretended hesitation, "Hmmm do I think we could use that? As a matter of fact, we could, thank you very much," I answered with great delight. We had learned a very wonderful lesson in life. God, in spite of our many shortcomings, was **our** Jehovah Jireh. We were not worthy of the least of His favors, yet the provider of the Old Testament had not changed. He desired and still desires to be known as Jehovah Jireh - the Lord our provider. What a wonderful opportunity and blessing it is in life when we can experience and know God by one of His many names.

4. No Water - Thirst

El Elyon = The Most High God

It is interesting to note that they began this trial by leaving the Wilderness of Sin and were led into Rephidim. Rephidim means the "desert place." Israel was led into the desert so they could understand how needy they were. They were thirsty people who did not understand their thirst. It is much like the book of Revelation records for us concerning the Laodicean Church; they believed they were rich and in need of nothing, when in God's perspective, they were blind, poor and naked (see Revelation 3:17). God in His faithfulness and His great longing to reveal Himself allowed them to be found in this place. It would be His great opportunity to reveal Himself to His people once again. In the place of the desert, He reveals Himself as El Elyon, the Most High God. He is the God that can take care of any problem. He is all powerful, and all knowing; there is nothing that can come between Him and His people, except for one thing. El Elyon was rejected. What was their statement, "Is the Lord among us or not?"(see Exodus 17:7). What did they seem to be saying? "There must not be a God that can save us, God is not all powerful, He is not here." On that day El Elyon - the most High God who wanted to take care of their every need - walked away unheard and unreceived in the camp of Israel. May we understand that regardless of the battle, disappointment or thirst, El Elyon, "the Most High God" is watching and waiting to reveal Himself to us.

5. The Golden Calf

Jehovah Tsidkenu = The Lord our Righteousness

One of the saddest portions of Scripture recorded for us about God's chosen people is found in this story. Moses, the man of God, ascended up the mountain to meet with God for His people. Immediately after Moses left, God's people entered into a time of great sin. When Moses was removed from the scene, it gave God the chance to reveal to Israel another aspect of His nature. They did not understand that in God's sovereign plan, God had planned to become their personal leader for a season. God, Himself, would be watching and weighing everything that they did. It was very important for God to allow Israel to understand that Moses was not their righteousness; God was their righteousness. In this story of the golden calf, Israel clearly missed a deeper relationship with their God. Each time we find ourselves separated from others (whether it be temporary or permanent), it is a fresh opportunity to meet with our God alone. There are no distractions and no false motives in this private, secret place of God. May we cherish these times of sweet fellowship with the Lord our righteousness. It was much easier for them to reject God by this name because they had already rejected the Most High God. We want to be those that allow God to reveal Himself to us every moment of our lives.

A number of years ago I stood before the casket of a very special person in my life. I considered it an honor to express what his life had meant to me in the eulogy speech. What had once been so real would soon become a memory; I knew that my words would conclude the final lines of his story while on earth.

My eyes filled with tears as I began to share how much I loved this precious man. With great difficulty, I spoke the words over his body that I wished and I longed that I could have shared with him face to face. I began to realize again that people are the most important thing in life, yet we are never guaranteed that we'll have tomorrow with them. I knew that God was revealing to me the importance of setting things straight and living a life that is loving and caring today. None of us can assume that we'll have another chance, another opportunity to express our thankfulness and love for those that have so freely given to us. That day as I stood before my father's casket, I knew that the words I so longingly wished to share with him I could never speak. May we not be those that live a life of rejecting, always believing that we will have another opportunity. I learned a very difficult and powerful lesson. If we live a life of waiting for tomorrow, we will still be waiting when there are no longer any tomorrows. However, if we live a life of living for today, when tomorrow comes it will not be too late. May we learn from the example I have shared about my father and also through the story of the golden calf, not to reject our opportunities to experience the character of God in our lives.

The name Jehovah Tsidkenu is to be whispered into our ear morning by morning as we realize that it is only by His righteousness that we have access and can walk through the trial of our "golden calves."

6. Complaining - Murmuring

Jehovah Rohi = The Lord is my Shepherd

Perhaps the most tender and gentle name we have in connection to God's names is Jehovah Rohi, The Lord is my Shepherd. This name carries the thought that God will instruct and lead us with His gentle hand. It is sad how often we miss the Lord in this aspect of His character. He was softly leading the children of Israel. His fire and His cloud led them and cared for them. They had food for their families, and their garments did not wear out. Yet, Israel who had Jehovah Rohi walking day after day with them, rejected Him as their shepherd. They began to complain and murmur about their lack of blessing rather than being thankful for the blessing they were living in. How often our perspective needs to change; we constantly look at our lack rather than our abundance. So many areas of the Christian walk can be summed up or understood by our perspective on life. If we were to receive what we really deserve, none of us could stand before the throne. The Bible states that we are all guilty and have gone astray. Yet, God in His mercy walks with us as Jehovah Rohi. He is the tender, gentle Shepherd who overlooks so many of our failings. We must realize that God longs to visit us in the midst of our difficulties. If we are refusing to accept our trials of life, then we are also refusing the One who created the trial. We want to fall in love with our Shepherd and the protector of His fold.

7. Ungratefulness by Mixed Multitude

Jehovah Raphe = God who Heals

The manna fell day after day, month after month. They ate manna for breakfast, manna for lunch, manna for dinner, manna for dessert. Why do you think God allowed them to be fed with only this manner of food? God could have provided them with filet mignon or the greatest feast known to man. Why didn't God provide in this fashion? He had a greater desire. God wanted to reveal Himself as Jehovah Raphe in the camp of Israel. As their hearts would ache, Jehovah Raphe, the God who heals, would come and heal their broken hearts. As they would complain and reject Jehovah Rohi, Jehovah Raphe would quickly rush in to heal the wounds. God was not interested in their short term comfort; He was interested in their eternal destiny. Manna was only the instrument used by God to touch the heart of every Israelite with something far deeper. It is the same in the Christian walk. The trial and the trouble are not important to God. Revealing Himself to us as Jehovah Raphe is important to God. He wants us to understand that He can come into our lives and heal every wound if we will allow Him to touch our lives in the midst of our wilderness. What a tragedy that Israel had missed this aspect of the Lord. May we learn to be those that are found walking out of our wilderness leaning on the Beloved.

8. Gluttony

Jehovah Nissi = The Lord my Banner

If Israel had known God by any name in their short history, this was a name that they seemingly had known and understood. He had been their banner. Jehovah Nissi had come to their defense; He had saved them and provided for them on every hand. Yet, what do we read in this eighth test? Upon receiving quail from God, Israel stuffed themselves with food. In fact, the Scripture records for us that the person who gathered the least gathered ten homers. Imagine that, a homer is estimated to be approximately five bushels. That means that these Israelites had gathered fifty bushels of quail and were not storing them for another day; they were gorging themselves with this meat. What were they saying? "Jehovah Nissi, You are not my banner any more". We will provide; we will look out for ourselves." Once again, the Israelites walked away from this trial rejecting another aspect of God's character. May we realize that it is only because of Jehovah Nissi, the Lord who fights our battles and is our banner, that any battle is won, and may we learn to fall in love with Jehovah Nissi, the Lord our Banner.

9. Criticism against Leaders

Jehovah Shammah = The Lord is There

This name was applicable to this trial and is also applicable to the church today. We can read about these trials and understand that Israel had rejected God, yet we must also understand that we are no different. Leaders are often maligned, rejected and criticized. In fact, I believe one of the greatest indictments against the Church is how we have treated our fallen leaders and comrades. Many have risen up, libeled and rejected certain brethren. The Church proclaims to the world that there is forgiveness and restoration, and yet we reject this very concept every day in the very churches that profess this belief. We must ask God to grip us with the truth that how we are treating the least of the brethren is literally how we are treating the Lord. This is the thought regarding Jehovah Shammah. God saw every accusation against Moses, and God sees every statement we make regarding leaders. This is not to say that leaders cannot make mistakes, they make many; but God sees and hears every word and action toward those whom He has sovereignly appointed. Jehovah Shammah walked in the midst of the camp of Israel, and Jehovah Shammah walks in the midst of the Church. The Lord is there. Our question should be: How do we treat Him?

10. Unbelief

Adonai = The Trinity

Finally, the last chapter had to be written. What had the Israelites done that was so terrible? Was it that they had failed nine trials? God longed to show them who He was, and in so doing He had finally revealed His very nature. The Father was revealed, the Son was revealed, and the Holy Spirit was revealed. Israel had rejected faith itself, and without faith it is impossible to inherit the land of Canaan. It was not their repeated sins that kept them from entering Canaan; it was their rejection of God Himself. It is not a matter of us crossing the line of no return; we cross this threshold daily. The problem was they had rejected the very God that alone could bring them in. May we be those that open our hearts and spirits to God as never before and throughout every trial see a fresh glimpse of the One that we love. That is always His purpose and is clearly seen in the ten trials of the wilderness and the many trials in our lives. May we choose to embrace God as He visits us and reveals His nature to us. May we be inspired to love Him and to love Him alone.

John will write to us for the rest of his letter about the character of love he has seen and heard: that all mature Christians are those who love others. This is what John had experienced while he walked with Christ for those three and a half years of complete renovation to all of his concepts and thoughts about what true godliness was to be. What he saw in the following story was, perhaps, the greatest story of love exhibited in the life of Christ.

Now before the feast of the Passover, when Jesus knew that His hour had come that He should depart from this world to the Father, having loved His own who were in the world, He loved them to the end. And supper being ended, the devil having already put it into the heart of Judas Iscariot, Simon's son, to betray Him, Jesus, knowing that the Father had given all things into His hands, and that He had come from God and was going to God, rose from supper and laid aside His garments, took a towel and girded Himself. After that, He poured water into a basin and began to wash the disciples' feet, and to wipe them with the towel with which He was girded. Then He came to Simon Peter. And Peter said to Him, "Lord, are You washing my feet? Jesus answered and said to him, "What I am doing you do not understand now, but you will know after this. Peter said to Him, "You shall never wash my feet!" Jesus answered him, "If I do not wash you, you have no part with Me. Simon Peter said to Him, "Lord, not my feet only, but also my hands and my head! Jesus said to him, "He who is bathed needs only to wash his feet, but is completely clean; and you are clean, but not all of you. For He knew who would betray Him; therefore He said, "You are not all clean. So when He had washed their feet, taken His garments, and sat down again, He said to them, "Do you know what I have done to you? You call me Teacher and Lord, and you say well, for so I am. If I then, your Lord and Teacher, have washed your feet, you also ought to wash one another's feet. For I have given you an example, that you should do as I have done to you. Most assuredly, I say to you, a servant is not greater than his master; nor is he who is sent greater than he who sent him. If you know these things, blessed are you if you do them. I do not speak concerning all of you. I know whom I have chosen; but that the Scripture may be fulfilled, 'He who eats bread with Me has lifted up his heel against Me.

> *Now I tell you before it comes, that when it does come to pass, you may believe that I am He. Most assuredly, I say to you, he who receives whomever I send receives Me; and he who receives Me receives Him who sent Me. (John 13:1-20)*

I am sure we have all asked ourselves, "How much of God's love am I required to reveal?" What do we see in Jesus' example? Jesus, knowing who Judas was, was still willing to wash the feet of His betrayer. Can you imagine what John must have thought or felt? "How can this be? The Lord of Glory is washing our feet!" Yet, Jesus was illustrating a point to them and to us. He was willing to stoop to the lowest degree to love. Jesus was found calling Judas "friend" in the Garden of Gethsemane. Jesus is willing to love all kinds. He risked His reputation with the religious leaders of His day to be found with lepers, sinners, Pharisees, adulterous women, the sick, the demon possessed, Roman soldiers, tax collectors, paralytics, rich and poor. There was no one exempt from the love of God.

The fact is that Jesus is still found ministering in the low places. He ministers to the drug addict, the alcoholic, the murderer, the AIDS patient. This is who Jesus is; it is not a fairy tale or a story in a book. *This is the life of Christ.* John had heard and seen a powerful example in Jesus' life, and he allowed it to change his life. When confronted with who Jesus really is, are we changed? When confronted with who Jesus really ministers to, will we minister to them also? When confronted with our ideas being radically altered, are we willing for them to be altered? Who is Jesus loving ***through you***?

Three Groups of Christians

1 John 2:12-14

I write to you, little children, Because your sins are forgiven you for His name's sake. I write to you, fathers, Because you have known Him who is from the beginning. I write to you, young men, Because you have overcome the wicked one. I write to you, little children, Because you have known the Father. I have written to you, fathers, Because you have known Him who is from the beginning. I have written to you, young men, Because you are strong, and the word of God abides in you, And you have overcome the wicked one.

Here we find John writing to us about three groups of Christians: children, young men and fathers. He had heard from the mouth of Jesus that there were to be three groups of Christians.

In the book of Matthew, they are referred to as those who are thirty-fold, sixty-fold, and hundred-fold. We will see that the Scripture very clearly gives us the understanding that there is an opportunity for maturity in the Christian walk. There are those who have yielded their hearts to God and have become overcomers. While there are also those who, though Christians, have rejected many of the dealings of God in their lives and have remained 30-fold or baby Christians.

"But others fell on good ground and yielded a crop: some a hundredfold, some sixty, some thirty. He who has ears to hear, let him hear! And the disciples came and said to Him, "Why do You speak to them in par-

ables?" He answered and said to them, "Because it has been given to you to know the mysteries of the kingdom of heaven, but to them it has not been given. For whoever has, to him more will be given, and he will have abundance; but whoever does not have, even what he has will be taken away from him. Therefore I speak to them in parables, because seeing they do not see, and hearing they do not hear, nor do they understand. And in them the prophecy of Isaiah is fulfilled, which says: 'Hearing you will hear and shall not understand, And seeing you will see and not perceive; For the hearts of this people have grown dull. Their ears are hard of hearing, And their eyes they have closed, Lest they should see with their eyes and hear with their ears, Lest they should understand with their hearts and turn, So that I should heal them.' "But blessed are your eyes for they see, and your ears for they hear;" (Matthew 13:8-16)

As a side note, have you ever wondered why Jesus did not allow certain people to understand His teaching? Why did He speak in parables? The answer lies within the mercy of God. Scripture tells us that we will be judged according to the truth we have received. It was merciful of God to keep them from understanding the truth they would have rejected anyway; therefore, their judgment was less severe. Then what about those who wanted to know the truth? The Lord knew that the hungry will always inquire. If we were to study the Gospel accounts of the parables, we would find Jesus always explaining - whether through further instruction or a natural circumstance - the meaning of His parables. He does not want us to be left with little or no insight. However, He is interested in preserving life and judgment. Truth is a very weighty thing to receive and a very weighty thing to give. So we must be careful with every word we speak because it will literally increase the judgment of those who hear it. This is why Jesus spoke in this manner; He realized the importance of His words. The hungry would inquire and receive instruction; and the hard-hearted would walk away without understanding and thereby incur a less severe judgment. Remember, the Bible does reveal that some will be beaten with many stripes and some with few (Luke 12:27,28). There is a difference in each man's judgment. Jesus was very careful in every word He spoke because He realized the importance of this truth.

Now let's look at the various positions we spoke of earlier. It is very clear in Scripture that some will overcome and others will enter God's Kingdom "as if by fire" (1 Corinthians 3:15). In any kingdom, there are kings, princes, and their subjects, which would include the thought of servants. Such is the Kingdom of Heaven and its various positions. Following is a small chart that lists a few of these examples; however, we must realize that there are multiplied examples of God's Kingdom order.

THE CHART OF MATURITY

Little Children	Young Men	Fathers
30-Fold	60-Fold	100-Fold
Called	Chosen	Faithful
Outer Court	Holy Place	Holy of Holies
First Heaven	Second Heaven	Third Heaven
Dew	Small Rain	Showers
Remnant	Bride	Manchild (Overcomers)

To help us better understand what this chart signifies, let's consider one of the topics; the Outer Court: Holy Place, and Holy of Holies. What does this mean? The Outer Court was the place where all Israel was welcome. Every Israelite could freely walk in the Outer Court, yet it was a distance away from the manifested presence of God that was found in the Holy of Holies. In the Christian walk, we can also experience the Outer Court where we are part of the Israelite nation, yet we do not avail ourselves of the Holy Place or the Holy of Holies. The following two sections of the Tabernacle were open to the priests or those that ministered to the Lord. The next place found is the Holy Place. The Levite, those servants who were the priests of God, came into the Holy Place where the candlestick and the table of shewbread were found. As we grow into maturity and begin truly serving the Lord (when we have come to the place that we realize whatever we do unto the least, we do unto Him), we are those that can then begin to walk into the Holy Place or a place of a deeper, sanctified life. The last place seen is the Holy of Holies. This was only accessible to the High Priest. The visible manifest presence of God was seen by this High Priest. This is the highest level of maturity in the Christian walk, where we are so much in love with God that we are those, who like Jesus, walk with and daily commune with the manifested presence of God. This should be the desire and hope of every Christian. So, we can see from this "shadow" and the examples that are to follow, that the Christian walk is to be a walk of constant maturity which God has clearly allowed us to see through all of Scripture and, again, through the writings of John.

There is a danger here that I feel we must guard ourselves from. These are positions that we can all attain to as Christians; however, our goal is simply to love the Lord and to allow Him to become the pleasure of our lives. There is a powerful example of someone in the Bible who wanted to attain the highest and was out of order - Satan himself. He wanted to be "like the Most High" (Isaiah 14:14). This is not to be our goal; our highest aspiration should be to become a loving friend of God.

We must be careful not to place God in a box where we declare before people and heaven, "If we do this for God, then He must respond this way." God is a sovereign God. He can forgive as often as He chooses and still speak blessing to one and judgment to another. Why is one person hundred-fold and another thirty-fold? When a person has chosen to follow God with all of his or her heart, it is still God's divine choice as to what they will become. The most important question here is not what we can or should be. As Jesus said to Peter concerning John the Beloved, "What is that to you? You follow Me" (John 21:22). Let's consider one final example given to us concerning this subject of allowing God to choose and maturity in Christ.

> *"For the kingdom of heaven is like a landowner who went out early in the morning to hire laborers for his vineyard. Now when he had agreed with the laborers for a denarius a day, he sent them into his vineyard. And he went out about the third hour and saw others standing idle in the marketplace, and said to them, 'You also go into the vineyard, and whatever is right I will give you.' So they went. Again he went out about the sixth and the ninth hour, and did likewise. And about the eleventh hour he went out and found others standing idle, and said to them, 'Why have you been standing here idle all day?' They said to him, 'Because no one hired us.' He said to them, 'You also go into the vineyard, and whatever is right you will receive.' So when evening had come, the owner of the vineyard said to his steward, 'Call the laborers and give them their wages, beginning with the last to the first.' And when those came who were hired about the eleventh hour, they each received a denarius. But when the first came, they supposed that they would receive more; and they likewise received each a denarius. And when*

> *they had received it, they complained against the land-owner, saying, 'These last men have worked only one hour, and you made them equal to us who have borne the burden and the heat of the day.' But he answered one of them and said, 'Friend, I am doing you no wrong. Did you not agree with me for a denarius? 'Take what is yours and go your way. I wish to give to this last man the same as to you. 'Is it not lawful for me to do what I wish with my own things? Or is your eye evil because I am good?' So the last will be first, and the first last. For many are called, but few chosen."*

This is a perfect example of what we so often see in the Church today. In fact, in regard to this specific portion of Scripture, there has been much false teaching. It is commonly taught that all those who are alive in the end, in the day of reward, will all receive the same. Nothing could be further from the truth. Paul writes to us that he fought the good fight of faith and **because of that**, there is laid up for him a crown of righteousness (2 Timothy 4:7,8). Reward is clearly linked with effort. No employer, general of an army, or superior of any kind would reward an unfaithful man. On the other hand, how much more will God, who sees and understands all, reward His faithful servants for their willingness to give their time and effort for His people?

What do we see in this section of Scripture? We would all agree that the first workers were hired to work for a certain amount and that the last workers were paid the same as the first. But the key question is, "Why were they paid the same?" Was it because of the goodness of God? Was this just a sovereign choice? I believe the rest of the story gives us the real answer and the clear picture. What is the response of the early workers when the wages are paid? "And when they had received it, they complained against the landowner, saying, "These last men have worked only one hour, and you made them equal to us who have borne the burden and heat of the day," (vs. 11,12). What was the problem here? These people still had a major weakness. They did not allow the "heat of the day" or the "burden" to do a work in their hearts. They were still murmurers and complainers. We know the landowner is a type of God the Father because Jesus started this parable with "The kingdom of heaven is like." We can see heavenly truths depicted in this natural story. As the landowner sought to teach his servants a lesson, God will also use circumstances to teach us and change us. They received the reward of a "baby Christian" because that is what they were. They were still babies complaining and murmuring over what others received rather than investigating and mourning over their own lives. Many Christians believe that going through trials and "burdens" will produce godliness. This is not necessarily always true. Many people endure the trials of life only to come out of them more bitter or hard-hearted. Many years ago the Lord spoke to me "trials do not build character, **embraced** trials build character."

One of the most important questions every Christian must answer is "Who will rule over my life?" We have the opportunity to let King Jesus rule and let Him decide for our lives. We can place our future into the hands of a loving Heavenly Father who will only choose what is best for us, or we can be those who remain "babies" in the Kingdom never accepting our circumstances and never growing into what God has intended for us. May we embrace God's trials and become mature sons in the Kingdom.

John is explaining to us that we as Christians have the opportunity to grow from "spiritual babyhood" (Christ in the manger) to "spiritual manhood" (Christ during His ministry) in His precious Kingdom. May the following Scripture inspire us to give our lives to the Lord of the Universe and allow Him to dictate our lives.

That we should no longer be children, tossed to and fro and carried about with every wind of doctrine, by the trickery of men, in the cunning craftiness of deceitful plotting, but, speaking the truth in love, may grow up in all things into Him who is the head; Christ. (Ephesians 4:14,15)

Love of the Father and the Love of the World

1 John 2:15-17

Do not love the world or the things in the world. If anyone loves the world, the love of the Father is not in him. For all that is in the world; the lust of the flesh, the lust of the eyes, and the pride of life; is not of the Father but is of the world. And the world is passing away, and the lust of it; but he who does the will of God abides forever.

From the Gospel of John, and, in fact, all of the Gospel accounts, we know that Jesus overcame the world. John could write with confidence because he had seen the Lord overcome every aspect and every temptation the world could offer. Not only had he seen this, but, he had also heard instruction from the Lord concerning this truth.

> *"Indeed the hour is coming, yes, has now come, that you will be scattered, each to his own, and will leave Me alone. And yet I am not alone, because the Father is with Me. These things I have spoken to you, that in Me you may have peace. In the world you will have tribulation; but be of good cheer, I have overcome the world." (John 16:32-33)*

Why did Jesus need to reassure us that He had overcome the world? Why would He warn us about tribulation that is found in the world? Many Christians choose to overlook this truth, but it is emphasized in the words of Jesus, "In the world ***you will have*** tribulation." I want to look at a few thoughts concerning this verse (referring to John 16:32-33) and John's statement.

Many people believe that Christians should be delivered from all hardships. Jesus has made it very clear that Christians will have troubles. It should be expected that, as we take a stand (as Jesus did) that is not popular with the world, we will be opposed. It should be expected that, as we lead our families in accordance with the Scripture, those in the world will not understand. That is what Jesus is saying. The conclusion of this verse is actually a promise to those who suffer. We, too, can overcome the world through the wisdom and the understanding of the Lord. I believe we can overcome naturally and spiritually, as we will see in the following paragraphs.

One small example of this is manifested as we raise our children. If we will follow God's way and the pattern He has established in Scripture, there is a blessing we can expect. Our children will be happy and functionally sound. In this day and age, when children do not respect or honor their parents, we can overcome the world - if we are willing to face the onslaught of the world and raise our children God's way. In every area of our lives, we will see this pattern of success repeated when we do things God's way. We must realize that His way always works; and the world's way will always diametrically oppose it.

The world's methods are not to be the church's methods. This leads us to the second issue we want to look at concerning the world. The epistle of John says it very plainly, "If anyone loves the world, the love of the Father is not in him." A major corruption has entered the Church. We run after the world to produce results. This is not the counsel of Scripture, rather, it is quite the opposite. Is this to say that we should live without electricity or without automobiles? This is not what is being said. In these verses, the word *world* can be better interpreted as "cosmos." It carries the thought of adorning or decoration. Where do we find this in the Church today? Many, many places! I want you to carefully consider a thought, not quickly, but carefully and deeply. Search your heart. If the Scripture revealed an area of your life that was in contradiction to God's way, would you change your way of thinking and acting? Most of us would say, "Why, of course." Let me give you one example of a truth that is consistently rejected by the Church: God's order for music. The Bible commands us to praise the Lord with a clap, with dance (David danced in the presence of the Lord), with hands lifted up, and with many other external expressions. Yet, in many churches (please realize, I am not attacking, only stating what I believe to be true), you would be removed from the church for any of these "offenses." Why? Because we do not allow the Scripture to determine our doctrine; but instead we are guided by the wisdom of the world and our own methods or thoughts. You might say, "No, we do not simply reject things, we have reasons for our actions." Yes, there is reasoning, and there is the Scripture. What does the Bible say? We must remember that each verse must be interpreted in the light of every other verse. We cannot take one verse and use it to refute another passage. All verses must work together to have pure doctrine. You cannot use the thought of "we do not want to be an offense," for example, and remove or excuse Scriptures you feel are offensive. ***All*** Scripture is given for correction, rebuke and instruction in righteousness (2 Timothy 3:16); not some, but all.

You might say that this is hard truth. We are living in hard days. The Bible warns us in Second Peter 3:3 "Knowing this first: that scoffers will come in the last days, walking according to ***their own*** lusts." The truth is, our opinions and our methods do not matter; only God's opinions and God's methods are truly life-giving and the only answer. Why allow the world to dictate our decisions when we serve a God that is loving, powerful and full of wisdom?

Is the Bible your final authority in all matters of faith and conduct? Is it the proving ground? John knew that only Christ in him could overcome the counsel of the world. He had faced this difficult decision. As they were about to drop him into a vat of boiling oil, John did not fear the oil of the world, for he had the anointing oil that can only come from Heaven. This precious anointing oil is available to us as we reject the world and its counsel and embrace the wisdom of Heaven.

The Backslidden Ex-comrade

1 John 2:18-20

Little children, it is the last hour; and as you have heard that the Antichrist is coming, even now many antichrists have come, by which we know that it is the last hour. They went out from us, but they were not of us; for if they had been of us, they would have continued with us; but they went out that they might be made manifest, that none of them were of us. But you have an anointing from the Holy One, and you know all things.

What a beautiful writer John was! He writes about those who had been part of the Kingdom at one time and have now gone after the ways of the world. He had become much like his Master, who often illustrated His teachings with a natural example. Two examples of this method are found in the Gospel of John. Jesus declares that He is the "light of the world" and then proceeds to give sight to the blind (John 9:5-7). He declares that He is the "bread of life" just after feeding the 5,000 (John 6:10,11,35). John had learned his lesson well. He will also now illustrate how those who love the world will ultimately fall away from their love relationship with the Father. He writes, "They went out from us," which would indicate that they were part at one time. He continues, "They were not of us," which would again indicate that they did not continue. He concludes, "Their decision was made manifest," which gives us the understanding that time will reveal what each person truly is. We can see the hope in

John with his concluding statement that the Holy Spirit can keep us.

John had seen this sad event happen; it was something he had witnessed and been a part of. Every Christian who has seen the falling away of an ex-comrade can only be grieved with this truth. John must have written this with much agony as he recalled the events of only a short time ago.

> *Therefore many of His disciples, when they heard this, said, "This is a hard saying; who can understand it?" When Jesus knew in Himself that His disciples complained about this, He said to them, "Does this offend you? What then if you should see the Son of Man ascend where He was before? It is the Spirit who gives life; the flesh profits nothing. The words that I speak to you are spirit, and they are life. But there are some of you who do not believe." For Jesus knew from the beginning who they were who did not believe, and who would betray Him. And He said, "Therefore I have said to you that no one can come to Me unless it has been granted to him by My Father." From that time many of His disciples went back and walked with Him no more. (John 6:60-66)*

How could this have happened? How could they walk away from the One who was full of truth and life? The answer lies with the desires of their heart; they sought the esteem of people. John had just finished writing about how the love of the Father and the love of the world do not mix, and now he illustrates it with this example. How could they walk away from the Lord? When the choice was to be made between God's opinion and theirs, they chose their own. It is one of the greatest dangers in wanting position or natural esteem. If we seek after anything other than God Himself, we are setting ourselves up for disappointment which will lend some to abandon the Kingdom altogether when their way is not satisfied. Our flesh will always fail; we must trust in mercy alone. To deny Christ, as they had done, we must forget one simple fact: we are the offender! How can we accuse others when we realize that we are the problem? There is a phrase that is used in the world today that carries a very negative connotation. It can be a terrible phrase at times and can cause much hurt and damage. Yet, there is a positive side to these words. We want to be "yes men" and "yes women." This desire should be in the heart of every Christian toward God. When God speaks, regardless of the personal sacrifice it may involve, we want to respond "Yes, Lord." When the Scripture contradicts our lives, we want to say, "Yes, Lord, I will change." John was also confronted with this difficult choice and responded properly although there were many things he did not understand. He knew that this itinerant preacher was more than a man, He was the Master and the Lord of his life. If others would leave the Lord and become ex-comrades, John would stay, regardless of the consequence. John would continue to be a comrade in arms.

> *But Simon Peter answered Him, "Lord, to whom shall we go? You have the words of eternal life. (John 6:68)*

Abiding with God

1 John 2:21-29

I have not written to you because you do not know the truth, but because you know it, and that no lie is of the truth. Who is a liar but he who denies that Jesus is the Christ? He is antichrist who denies the Father and the Son. Whoever denies the Son does not have the Father either; he who acknowledges the Son has the Father also. Therefore let that abide in you which you heard from the beginning. If what you heard from the beginning abides in you, you also will abide in the Son and in the Father. And this is the promise that He has promised us; eternal life. These things I have written to you concerning those who try to deceive you. But the anointing which you have received from Him abides in you, and you do not need that anyone teach you; but as the same anointing teaches you concerning all things, and is true, and is not a lie, and just as it has taught you, you will abide in Him. And now, little children, abide in Him, that when He appears, we may have confidence and not be ashamed before Him at His coming. If you know that He is righteous, you know that everyone who practices righteousness is born of Him.

The thought of abiding is mentioned six times in the Gospel of John. The word *abide* means "to remain as one, not to become another or different." It is the same word that is used to describe the oneness between a husband and wife. We have already seen that the love of God was revealed to us in the very beginning of time as God gave life to those who would someday take life from His only Son. We cannot abide with Him unless we have this love working in us toward others. Consider what John was saying in these verses found in his Gospel. How can we attain to that place of oneness?

I have come as a light into the world, that whoever believes in Me should not abide in darkness. (John 12:46)

And I will pray the Father, and He will give you another Helper, that He may abide with you forever; (John 14:16)

Abide in Me, and I in you. As the branch cannot bear fruit of itself, unless it abides in the vine, neither can you, unless you abide in Me. (John 15:4)

If anyone does not abide in Me, he is cast out as a branch and is withered; and they gather them and throw them into the fire, and they are burned. (John 15:6)

If you abide in Me, and My words abide in you, you will ask what you desire, and it shall be done for you. (John 15:7)

If you keep My commandments, you will abide in My love, just as I have kept My Father's commandments and abide in His love. (John 15:10)

While reading these verses, we should come to at least one conclusion: we cannot abide based on our own ability or our own strength. Every verse reveals our need of help from someone or from God Himself. How can we receive this help? A fully revealed Christ can only bring forth a perfect man. The Lord must be complete in each church in order for us to have pure doctrine and pure fellowship. That is quite obvious; yet how can we have Christ fully formed (or revealed) in us? The Scripture tells us that Jesus spoke many "hard sayings" to the multitudes. Often His words would bring conviction, correction and a call to self-denial. Likewise, we see the words of Paul carry the same message. Many Christians would like to deny the following portion of Paul's writing. Surely, this is a place where Paul's opinion was wrong. Surely, Paul must have made a mistake here. How can we have a fully revealed Christ? There is only one way according to Scripture.

> *And He Himself gave some to be apostles, some prophets, some evangelists, and some pastors and teachers, for the equipping of the saints for the work of ministry, for the edifying of the body of Christ, till we all come to the unity of the faith and of the knowledge of the Son of God, to a perfect man, to the measure of the stature of the fullness of Christ; that we should no longer be children, tossed to and fro and carried about with every wind of doctrine, by the trickery of men, in the cunning craftiness of deceitful plotting. (Ephesians 4:11-14)*

God has ordained the five-fold ministry (apostle, prophet, evangelist, pastor and teacher) to enable His people to come to a place of maturity and perfection. The only way that we can attain this place of abiding and becoming one with Him is by placing our lives under the ministry of God's choosing. This is not to say that all ministry is perfect; however, that is far from the issue. The thought is that *in spite* of a pastor's shortcomings, God will use him to produce something that is eternal in you. In fact, it may be his very shortcomings which are used to produce something godly in you. We do not submit to a man, we submit to the office that God has ordained. There is no other way to have a fully revealed Christ without the five-fold ministry. That is what the Bible declares. Now, while all of the pastors and leaders are shouting "Amen," let's consider the leader's responsibility. A pastor cannot fulfill this place of anointing by himself; this is a five-fold ministry. He needs the help of the apostle, teacher, evangelist, and prophet. A prophet cannot fulfill this unity of the faith on his own; he needs the help of the pastor, apostle, evangelist and teacher. This is the reason that cross-pollination is so important in our churches. A church full of teachers can only produce teachers, but a church full of all of the gifts can function properly and completely. If we find that we are void of certain gifts in our churches, we must then find those (men of uprightness) who are willing to come to our churches and leave a spiritual blessing. We can only abide with Christ when we have Christ fully. The word *abide* itself implies oneness, and the body of Christ can only be one as we are willing to allow each member of the body to fulfill his or her purpose.

Chapter 4

BECOMING LIKE THE ONE WE SEE

FIRST JOHN 3

1 JOHN 3:1-3

The more time we spend with someone, the more we will become like that person. The same is true with the Lord.

> *Behold what manner of love the Father has bestowed on us, that we should be called children of God! Therefore the world does not know us, because it did not know Him. Beloved, now we are children of God; and it has not yet been revealed what we shall be, but we know that when He is revealed, we shall be like Him, for we shall see Him as He is. And everyone who has this hope in Him purifies himself, just as He is pure.*

We are given a key here that we must not forget. We will be like Him, as He is revealed to us. Jesus must be revealed to us before we can be like Him. In the writing of

John's Gospel, we are given understanding about how Christ can be revealed. It is, in actuality, perhaps the most repulsive thought in the New Testament. It was so repulsive that many of the disciples left Jesus because of the hardness of this saying, yet this is what John had seen and heard. It was probably even difficult for John to receive the words of Jesus. What did John hear?

> *Jesus therefore answered and said to them, "Do not murmur among yourselves. No one can come to Me unless the Father who sent Me draws him; and I will raise him up at the last day. It is written in the prophets, 'And they shall all be taught by God.' Therefore everyone who has heard and learned from the Father comes to Me. Not that anyone has seen the Father, except He who is from God; He has seen the Father. Most assuredly, I say to you, he who believes in Me has everlasting life. I am the bread of life. Your fathers ate the manna in the wilderness, and are dead. This is the bread which comes down from heaven, that one may eat of it and not die. I am the living bread which came down from heaven. If anyone eats of this bread, he will live forever; and the bread that I shall give is My flesh, which I shall give for the life of the world. The Jews therefore quarreled among themselves, saying, "How can this Man give us His flesh to eat?" Then Jesus said to them, "Most assuredly, I say to you, unless you eat the flesh of the Son of Man and drink His blood, you have no life in you. "Whoever eats My flesh and drinks My blood has eternal life, and I will raise him up at the last day. For My flesh is food indeed, and My blood is drink indeed. He who eats My flesh and drinks My blood abides in Me, and I in him. As the living Father sent Me, and I live because of the Father, so he who*

> *feeds on Me will live because of Me. This is the bread which came down from heaven; not as your fathers ate the manna, and are dead. He who eats this bread will live forever." These things He said in the synagogue as He taught in Capernaum.*

How repulsive these statements were to those who had no understanding of their meaning. Many of them must have thought: "This can't be so, the book of Deuteronomy clearly declares to us that we cannot eat the blood" (Deuteronomy 12:33). Was Jesus in contradiction to the Scripture? Jesus had already given understanding of what the bread of life is: it is every word that proceeds from the mouth of God (Matthew 4:4). How sad that these disciples who had walked with Him for all of those years did not understand that it was only His words that gave them life. In the writings of Paul in Second Corinthians 2:3, we read "Who also hath made us able ministers of the new testament; not of the letter, but of the spirit: for the letter killeth, but the spirit giveth life." It is interesting to note, the word "*letter*" here is actually defined as "Scripture." In other words, he is writing to us that the Scripture killeth. Many would strongly object to this concept. However, this is what the Scripture itself actually declares. Jesus, Himself, said that the Pharisees searched the Scriptures because they thought they could find life in them, yet it is only in Him that we can find true life (John 5:39). Let's consider a few examples from the Scripture to illustrate our point and then conclude with the thought of becoming like the one we see.

Abraham was enjoying life in the Kingdom of God. He was in Canaan. He had a wonderful son. He was called the "Father of the Multitude" Suddenly a voice spoke, "Abraham, take your son and sacrifice him on the altar." What would you have thought if you were Abraham? This was his beloved son. This was the heir to the promise. There was no promise without this son. If he were to slay him upon the altar, then Abraham could kiss all of his future good-bye. "Wait a minute," Abraham must have thought, "this can't be God!" God had written in the covenant with Noah, that if blood was shed, then that same man who shed the blood must be put to death. God's command to Abraham seemed to conflict with the covenant of Noah. Did this mean Abraham's obedience to God's voice would require him to violate the covenant of Noah? What a wonderful opportunity for Abraham to sidestep the voice of God. Yet, Abraham was a man of relationship. He knew it was God who was speaking. He knew that he had only one choice and that was to obey God, and God could choose to redeem the life of his son, Isaac. We know from the story of Abraham that God spared Isaac's life, but we also know that Abraham took him, placed him on the altar, and was ready to slay him when God finally spoke again. How could Abraham have this kind of faith? Because Abraham was not a man whose life was dictated by the written law, Abraham was a man of relationship who walked as God directed.

David was also a man of relationship; he is called a "man after God's own heart." There are at least four times in the life of David that he should have lost his life: he ate the shewbread, he went before the ark, he killed Uriah, and he committed adultery with Bathsheba. He broke the law in all of these offenses and deserved death. Yet Nathan, in his own pronunciation of the judgment of God, redeemed the life of David. Why? Why did God seemingly violate His own law? He never did! He only violated ***our*** law or ***our*** understanding of the law! We place the law over the lives of men, but God has always placed the broken and contrite spirit of a man (a repentant life) over His law. David was one who was seeking God, and who was broken before God. He was a man who was full of failure, yet he was a man that in the midst of his failure sought God. God will never reject nor cast out this type of man. In fact, this is exactly the kind of man that God is looking for. Why was David not judged? He was a man of relationship, not a man of law.

Note: For those who feel David was wrong to eat the shewbread, Jesus Himself defended David's actions in the Gospel (Matthew 12:3,4).

Isaiah is another example of a man of relationship. We know that Isaiah was a prophet of God. He heard the voice of God and delivered the message to the people. Isaiah was also a man that defended, supported, and judged the keeping of the law as any of the prophets were required to do. This did not hinder Isaiah's relationship; it only enhanced it. Consider a word that Isaiah received in Isaiah 20:1-3. He was told to walk *naked* for three years. He could have explained this away. "This is not God. God would never ask me to lose my dignity, and to abase my prophetic office." Isaiah knew that it was God. How? He knew the voice of God and understood that his relationship with God was the most important thing in life. His reputation and personal discomfort were not important; his understanding and obedience to God's voice was.

Jesus, of course, is the perfect and ultimate example and test for any doctrine. If our doctrine cannot be found in His life, it is incorrect doctrine. We have already stated that He has declared that there is only life in Him. In His earthly ministry, we find the Pharisees constantly attacking Him. Their main reason was they felt He was in violation of the Scripture. Let's consider one example to illustrate what we are saying.

After this there was a feast of the Jews, and Jesus went up to Jerusalem. Now there is in Jerusalem by the Sheep Gate a pool, which is called in Hebrew,

Bethesda, having five porches. In these lay a great multitude of sick people, blind, lame, paralyzed, waiting for the moving of the water. For an angel went down at a certain time into the pool and stirred up the water; then whoever stepped in first, after the stirring of the water, was made well of whatever disease he had. Now a certain man was there who had an infirmity thirty-eight years. When Jesus saw him lying there, and knew that he already had been in that condition a long time, He said to him, "Do you want to be made well?" The sick man answered Him, "Sir, I have no man to put me into the pool when the water is stirred up; but while I am coming, another steps down before me." Jesus said to him, "Rise, take up your bed and walk." And immediately the man was made well, took up his bed, and walked. And that day was the Sabbath. The Jews therefore said to him who was cured, "It is the Sabbath; it is not lawful for you to carry your bed." He answered them, "He who made me well said to me, 'Take up your bed and walk.'" (John 5:1-11)

I love the explanation to this story! Can you imagine the audacity of the Pharisees to accuse Jesus, the law giver, of violating the law? According to the law of Moses, no man was to carry a burden on the Sabbath. The mistake that the Pharisees were making was that this man no longer had a burden. It was the first time in 38 years that his bed **was not** an encumbrance. Much to the contrary, it was a delight for him to carry that bed. He must have walked down the street rejoicing that his true burden had been lifted. Jesus was not in violation of the law! He had come to release the burden of the law! How God's heart must long for a people that will love Him and daily commune with Him as friend to friend. The Pharisees were so determined to follow the law with such rigidity that they missed the Savior when He walked among them. God is looking for a people that will live for Him, walk with Him and hear from Him.

In conclusion, there is only one way to become like the One we love. It is to spend time in the presence of God. As we kneel in the throne room of God looking at the Lamb that sits upon the throne, we will become like this gentle Lamb that will be sent to the nations (Isaiah 15:1). As we stand with the worshippers of Heaven, lifting our hands and raising our voice to the King, we will also become true worshippers offering thanksgiving and adoration to the King. Most importantly, we must become those who are lovers of God. As we love Him, we can trust the Scripture to be a further and a deeper revelation of His nature, character and life. This is not a demeaning of the Bible, only a deeper insight into what the Scripture has come to reveal. May we become like the one we see in the Scripture and the one we see daily walking in our midst.

The Message of Love (Part 2)

1 John 3:4-24

Whoever commits sin also commits lawlessness, and sin is lawlessness. And you know that He was manifested to take away our sins, and in Him there is no sin. Whoever abides in Him does not sin. Whoever sins has neither seen Him nor known Him. Little children, let no one deceive you. He who practices righteousness is righteous, just as He is righteous. He who sins is of the devil, for the devil has sinned from the beginning. For this purpose the Son of God was manifested, that He might destroy the works of the devil. Whoever has been born of God does not sin, for His seed remains in him; and he cannot sin, because he has been born of God. In this the children of God and the children of the devil are manifest: Whoever does not practice righteousness is not of God, nor is he who does not love his brother. For this is the message that you heard from the beginning, that we should love one another, not as Cain who was of the wicked one and murdered his brother. And why did he murder him? Because his works were evil and his brother's righteous. Do not marvel, my brethren, if the world hates you. We know that we have passed from death to life, because we love the brethren. He who does not love his brother abides in death. Whoever hates his brother is a murderer, and you know that no murderer has eternal life abiding in him. By this we know love, because He laid down His life for us. And we also ought to lay down our lives for the brethren. But whoever has this world's goods, and sees his brother in need, and shuts up his heart from him, how does the love of God abide in him? My little children, let us not love in word or in tongue, but in deed and in truth. And by this we know that we are of the truth, and shall assure our hearts before Him. For if our heart condemns us, God is greater than our heart, and knows all things. Beloved, if our heart does not condemn us, we have confidence toward God. And whatever we ask we receive from Him, because we keep His commandments and do those things that are pleasing in His sight. And this is His commandment: that we should believe on the name of His Son Jesus Christ and love one another, as He gave us commandment. Now he who keeps His commandments abides in Him, and He in him. And by this we know that He abides in us, by the Spirit whom He has given us.

Let's begin looking at this section of Scripture by asking ourselves a few questions. If we were to answer, honestly, the following questions, what would our answers be? Remember, do not answer according to the topic of this chapter, but answer according to what you honestly believe - and more importantly, how you honestly live.

Of the following verses, which is the most important?

o *In the beginning was the Word, and the Word was with God, and the Word was God.* (John 1:1)

o *Jesus answered and said to him, "Most assuredly, I say to you, unless one is born again, he cannot see the kingdom of God."* (John 3:3)

o *Jesus said to him, " 'You shall love the LORD your God with all your heart, with all your soul, and with all your mind.' "This is the first and great commandment. And the second is like it: 'You shall love your neighbor as yourself.'* (Matthew 22:37-39)

o *I beseech you therefore, brethren, by the mercies of God, that you present your bodies a living sacrifice, holy, acceptable to God, which is your reasonable service.* (Romans 12:1)

o *Not with the blood of goats and calves, but with His own blood He entered the Most Holy Place once for all, having obtained eternal redemption.* (Hebrews 9:12)

What is the most important doctrine in the Bible?

o Sanctification
o Virgin Birth
o Baptism of Water
o Love
o Repentance
o End Times
o Authority
o Salvation
o Holy Spirit
o Justification

Who is the most spiritual person (besides Jesus) in the Bible, and why do you believe this?

What is the most spiritual act done by a person (besides Jesus) in the Bible, and why do you believe this?

Who do you believe is the most spiritual person you presently know, and why do you believe this?

____

____

____

____

____

____

These questions can and must only be evaluated in the light of all of the Scripture. The Bible clearly gives us understanding as to what is the most important doctrine. We are assured of this by the sayings of Jesus and by the backing of every writer of the New Testament.

Let me preface this by saying that if we do not accept the authority of the Scripture or the authority of God, it will be impossible for us to accept the truth. We must be rooted soundly in His authority to receive any commands from His throne. The whole premise of a command is founded upon the authority of the command giver. We must be those in submission to the Head to receive the command of this authority.

If we were to ask ourselves, "Who are the five most important witnesses in the New Testament?" I believe we would all answer the same - Jesus, Paul, Peter, John, and James. All five of these witnesses agree on the most fundamental doctrine in the Bible.

Jesus: *Jesus said to him, " 'You shall love the LORD your God with all your heart, with all your soul, and with all your mind.' This is the* ***first*** *and* ***great*** *commandment. And the second is like it: 'You shall love your neighbor as yourself.'* (Matthew 22:37-39)

Paul: *Owe no one anything except to love one another, for he who loves another has fulfilled the law. For the commandments, You shall not commit adultery, You shall not murder, You shall not steal, You shall not bear false witness, You shall not covet, and if there is any other commandment, are all summed up in this saying, namely, You shall love your neighbor as yourself. Love does no harm to a neighbor; therefore love is the fulfillment of the law.* (Romans 13:8-10)

Peter: *Since you have purified your souls in obeying the truth through the Spirit in sincere love of the brethren, love one another fervently with a pure heart.* (1 Peter 1:22)

John: *For this is the message that you heard from the beginning, that we should love one another.* (1 John 3:11)

James: *If you really fulfill the royal law according to the Scripture, You shall love your neighbor as yourself," you do well.* (James 2:8)

Loving the Lord and our neighbor is the most important doctrine in the Scripture. It is wonderful that Jesus answered this question so directly and clearly. We cannot dispute this thought. We cannot say, "That is your opinion and open to interpretation," because Jesus Himself said it. Consider how strongly Christians feel about certain doctrines in the Scripture. If someone would say that they did not believe the Virgin Birth or in the cleansing power of the blood, every Christian would rise up and defend their beliefs even unto death. How much more should we live and die for this, the most important of all doctrines. The greatest commandment that is given is the commandment to love one another. John knew that love would keep us in or out of the presence of God. God Himself is love, and only those who live in love can live in His presence. In the Gospel of John, we can see and understand the reason the Father loved the Son. It is for one reason: He loved the Son because He laid down His life for others.

> *"I am the good shepherd. The good shepherd gives His life for the sheep. But a hireling, he who is not the shepherd, one who does not own the sheep, sees the wolf coming and leaves the sheep and flees; and the wolf catches the sheep and scatters them. The hireling flees because he is a hireling and does not care about the sheep. I am the good shepherd; and I know My sheep, and am known by My own. As the Father knows Me, even so I know the Father; and I lay down My life for the sheep. And other sheep I have which are not of this fold; them also I must bring, and they will hear My voice; and there will be one flock and one shepherd. Therefore My Father loves Me, because I lay down My life that I may take it again. No one takes it from Me, but I lay it down of Myself. I have power to lay it down, and I have power to take it again. This command I have received from My Father." (John 10:11-18)*

As we lay down our lives for others, we will find ourselves in the presence of God. The most important truth I believe that God has ever revealed to me, I want to share with you in the next few sentences. There is nothing deeper that I can share and nothing deeper that I possess. We are told that the moment we become born-again, Christ comes and lives within each one of us. Regardless of the maturity of each Christian, we know that Christ is still found within each Christian. We are also told that Jesus is the mediator between God and men in First Timothy 2:5, *"For there is one God and one Mediator between God and men, the Man*

Christ Jesus". Jesus also tells us that if anyone rejects Him, He will also reject them before the Father (Mark 8:38).

Now, how does this all fit together? If we reject our brother (whom Christ is living within), then we are rejecting Christ. Our prayer life and our relationship with the Father is directly linked to our relationship with our fellow believers. Many prayers have come before the Son that must be rejected because of the bitterness or lack of submission to others in the Body of Christ. Our love relationship with the Father is directly related to how we treat others in the Body of Christ. When we reject Christ in the brethren, we must also be rejected in Heaven. We might ask, how much do we have to love? If we were able to spend a few moments in the shoes of John, how do you think he would answer this question? What had John seen and heard regarding the love of Christ?

> *Then, when Mary came where Jesus was, and saw Him, she fell down at His feet, saying to Him, Lord, if You had been here, my brother would not have died." Therefore, when Jesus saw her weeping, and the Jews who came with her weeping, He groaned in the spirit and was troubled. And He said, "Where have you laid him?" They said to Him, "Lord, come and see." Jesus wept. Then the Jews said, "See how He loved him!" And some of them said, "Could not this Man, who opened the eyes of the blind, also have kept this man from dying?" (John 11:32-38)*

In this account of Lazarus, we receive a wonderful story of love. It is not His raising of Lazarus that reveals His great love, but it is the story before the story. We can often read over some of the most important truths by reading ahead and not asking for understanding for every word of the

Scripture. Why do you think Jesus wept? It is the shortest verse in the English Bible and may carry the deepest truth. He knew that He was going to raise Lazarus from the dead, that's why He came. So, why was He crying? If we were going to raise a man from the dead, don't you think we would be shouting, dancing and rejoicing? Maybe it was because of the unbelief manifested here; but He had seen unbelief before and had not been reduced to tears. Why then was He crying? The Bible tells us the answer if we have a heart to understand. Upon seeing Jesus weeping, the reply of the people was, "See how He loved him." Why was Jesus crying? Because ***even one moment*** away from the heart of God hurts the one who loves so deeply. Christ is touched by *one missed opportunity* we could have had in His presence. He had come to the town of Bethany, and though He knew Lazarus would be with Him again shortly, He missed the presence of His friend. This is to be the heart of every Christian. This to be our heart toward every brother and sister in Christ. It is what John had seen and what John had heard. He writes so boldly and so confidently about the love of Christ because he ***knew*** that ***God is love.***

Chapter 5

TRUTH, LOVE AND WITNESS

FIRST JOHN 4

UNDERSTANDING THE SPIRIT OF TRUTH AND ERROR

1 JOHN 4:1-6

Beloved, do not believe every spirit, but test the spirits, whether they are of God; because many false prophets have gone out into the world. By this you know the Spirit of God: Every spirit that confesses that Jesus Christ has come in the flesh is of God, and every spirit that does not confess that Jesus Christ has come in the flesh is not of God. And this is the spirit of the Anti-christ, which you have heard was coming, and is now already in the world. You are of God, little children, and have overcome them, because He who is in you is greater than he who is in the world. They are of the world. Therefore they speak as of the world, and the world hears them. We are of God. He who knows God hears us; he who is not of God does not hear us. By this we know the spirit of truth and the spirit of error.

John now gives us the key to understanding the spirit of truth and the spirit of error. Those who truly know God will recognize and respond to God *in us*. It is interesting to note that they must hear ***us*** if they are to know God. It is not the ability to hear an audible voice from Heaven that John is writing about, but hearing God's voice through the brethren. They must hear ***us***. God speaks through donkeys, men like Balaam and Saul and many others in the Bible. We may see a person as an unworthy and unclean vessel, but God may see them as a perfect channel of His choice. We must understand that it is not the *ability of the messenger* that we are to center our lives upon, but it is instead *God's ability to speak* through **any** vessel.

The Pharisees were a perfect example of those who rejected the word of the Lord because they were not willing to receive the source through which it came. When Jesus, the Son of God, came in the flesh to speak the most powerful message the world had ever known, they were quick to reject Him because He was born of the flesh. "We are not born of fornication," they replied to Jesus (John 8:41). They were always looking at the flesh. They also, because of their unwillingness to receive from others, hindered the true message (the message of Christ) for their lives. There is a powerful story in connection with this thought found in the book of Luke. Let's read this story together to perhaps gain a deeper understanding of how God will and can use a natural man to carry His message. May we take heed to the warning that we as men can bypass the spirit of truth by rejecting God's earthly messengers.

So He came to Nazareth, where He had been brought up. And as His custom was, He went into the synagogue on the Sabbath day, and stood up to read. And He was handed the book of the prophet Isaiah. And when He had opened the book, He found the place where it was written: "The Spirit of the LORD is upon Me, Because He has anointed Me To preach the gospel to the poor; He has sent Me to heal the brokenhearted, To proclaim liberty to the captives And recovery of sight to the blind, To set at liberty those who are oppressed; To proclaim the acceptable year of the LORD." Then He closed the book, and gave it back to the attendant and sat down. And the eyes of all who were in the synagogue were fixed on Him. And He began to say to them, "Today this Scripture is fulfilled in your hearing. So all bore witness to Him, and marveled at the gracious words which proceeded out of His mouth. And they said, "Is this not Joseph's son?" He said to them, "You will surely say this proverb to Me, 'Physician, heal yourself! Whatever we have heard done in Capernaum, do also here in Your country.'" Then He said, "Assuredly, I say to you, no prophet is accepted in his own country. But I tell you truly, many widows were in Israel in the days of Elijah, when the heaven was shut up three years and six months, and there was a great famine throughout all the land; but to none of them was Elijah sent except to Zarephath, in the region of Sidon, to a woman who was a widow. And many lepers were in Israel in the time of Elisha the prophet, and none of them was cleansed except Naaman the Syrian." (Luke 4:16-27)

Jesus came to Nazareth to preach perhaps the most powerful words ever spoken to mankind. He was going to heal the broken-hearted, restore sight to the blind, set at liberty those who were oppressed, preach the gospel to the poor, and proclaim the acceptable year of the Lord. His message started out so wonderfully; the response of the people was very favorable. We can read that they all marveled at the gracious words He spoke. But then something happened, something terrible, something puzzling and yet something so alarming that ultimately these people, who a few moments earlier were marveling, are now ready to put Him to death. What happened? What caused this kind of response? What did He say? What did He do? Scripture makes it explicitly clear that it was nothing He had done or said. It was *who He was* that made them angry. It is recorded for us: "Is this not Joseph's son?" In today's English, we would say, "Wait a minute, how can He speak this way, He's only a man like us. Who does this guy think He is to speak as if He has the word of God? We remember Him when He was a baby. We remember Him when He was raised in our synagogue. Who does He think He is?" They missed the most powerful words ever spoken because they were not willing to look past the fleshly body of Jesus and receive the words of God through a spiritual man.

This scene in Nazareth concludes with Jesus speaking of a widow and Naaman. I often wondered, why did He choose two seemingly unrelated circumstances and people? What was so significant about their lives? As always, once the Lord gave understanding, the answer was so obvious and so simple. What was consistent in these two lives? What linked them together with what was happening in Nazareth? We know the illustration Jesus used concerned two Gentiles which must have infuriated the Israelites, but maybe there is another explanation for their wrath. The widow had a preconceived idea when Elijah came to town. We are told that she and her son were going to eat their last meal together and then die. What an unusual request, she must have thought, that this prophet would ask her to give up her last meal. Most of us would have found it very difficult to relinquish our meager supply: but this woman had a special quality; she was willing to change her preconceived ideas and allow the Lord to do a work through a man to preserve her life.

What about the man called Naaman? He had a perfect plan for his healing. The man of God would come and lay hands on him, and he would be healed. But Naaman would also have a surprise in store - God was going to work in a completely different way. Naaman was going to have to go and dip himself in a dirty, murky river in order to be healed. He also had to change his preconceived idea and allow the Lord to do a work through a different method than he had planned.

How often we miss the Lord because of our preconceived ideas! We believe that God can only speak through this man or through that vessel and consequently we miss the Lord entirely. Many will stand before the Lord with areas of defeat and weakness in their lives, only to find out that deliverance had come but they were too busy looking at the flesh (or fault of the vessel) to listen; therefore they walked in error.

How can we know the spirit of truth and the spirit of error? It is forever linked to our ability to hear God through His chosen vessel. Remember, God's instrument is not our choice and never will be our choice. It is the choice of God. Our only hope of walking in truth and not in error is to begin to open our ears as never before to God speaking to us through others. John saw and heard this personally. He knew this lesson well. May we be willing to change our preconceived ideas about those around us and allow our ears to hear and receive the words of heaven.

THE MESSAGE OF LOVE (PART III)

1 JOHN 4:7-11

Beloved, let us love one another, for love is of God; and everyone who loves is born of God and knows God. He who does not love does not know God, for God is love. In this the love of God was manifested toward us, that God has sent His only begotten Son into the world, that we might live through Him. In this is love, not that we loved God, but that He loved us and sent His Son to be the propitiation for our sins. Beloved, if God so loved us, we also ought to love one another.

Once again, John is illustrating and writing to us about the message of love. John could not escape this message; it had become his heart, his words, and his life. He had seen the Lord Jesus Christ give His life in love for the multitudes and for each individual in such a way that John was forever changed. Jesus, the Bridegroom, had come to earth to reveal His love for His Bride. He had begun His ministry with a wedding to indicate to all that the Bridegroom had come (see John 2:1-11). Now John would write about the love that this Bridegroom would reveal, the love that would ultimately cost the heavenly Bridegroom His life.

John writes that the Son was sent to be the propitiation for our sins. What does the word *propitiation* mean? It comes from the term "mercy seat," the cover of the ark which was sprinkled with the blood of the sacrificed animal on the annual Day of Atonement. This act signified that the life of the people - the loss of which they had merited by their own sins - was offered to God in the blood of the victim. It was by this act that their sins were forgiven, satisfying the justice of

God. This is the work of the Cross. Jesus came as a sinless man and died the death of the Cross in order that the debt of all sin might be forgiven - His blood sprinkled on the mercy seat. What a priceless gift we were given by the precious Lamb of God. However, John does not conclude this thought about the Son with what ***He*** gave. Instead, he challenges us with tenderness and directness, "*Beloved, if God so loved us, we also ought to love one another.*" In other words, we are to love as He loved; we are to lay down our lives in love for others as Jesus did. It is unlike *Phileo* love, which means in the Greek, "brotherly love." This degree of love basically says "You scratch my back and I'll scratch yours." Rather, it is the thought of *agape* love, which is love so intense that we would die for one another. This love expects nothing in return. If we will ever love as God loved, we will have this agape love working in our lives.

I want to share a thought here that is very important. The world will be won to the love of Christ when they *see* the love of Christ in us. It is no small wonder that in First Corinthians 13:13 we can read, "*And now abide faith, hope, love, these three; but the greatest of these is love.*" Love is found before faith and hope. In general the Church has missed the greatest key in the Scripture to winning the lost. It is not quoting the Romans road that will lead people to the Lord. Jesus was first and foremost a man of intense love for His people. For generations parents have played the game with their children where one will say, "How much do you love me?" and the reply is made with arms extended, "This much!" Someone has allegorically posed the question to Jesus, "How much do You love us?" His reply? He stretched out His arms on the cross and died. God's intent is for us to love as Jesus loved. If we will simply show people that we care, really care about them, then our witness will come out of our lives and not out of obligation or impure motives. The thought of soul-winning must be founded in love first.

I would like discuss briefly on winning others to the Lord. This is not an exhaustive study. Though we will give some small answers, we must remember the word of the Lord is our greatest resource. Remember, Jesus' words to Nicodemus were not the same words to the rich young ruler. We need to understand what God is saying to each individual. Let's consider a few small steps that might help us share Christ with others.

PRACTICAL WAYS TO WIN THE LOST

1. Love, Love, Love

Without love, we are as sounding brass and a clanging cymbal. We have just read that the greatest key is love. Many unbelievers have known the devoted love of a mother's heart or the love of a spouse. Once a person has experienced an expression of true love, they will be able to discern whether our love is genuine or hypocritical. They will recognize if we are out to add to our own cause, or if we are truly concerned about their lives. We must be kind and friendly. Below is a poem I read a number of years ago.

It costs nothing, but creates much. It enriches those who receive it,

without impoverishing those who give it.

It happens in a flash and the memory of it sometimes lasts forever.

None are so rich that they can get along without it, and none so poor but are richer for its benefits.

It fosters good will in a business and it creates happiness in the home.

It is the evidence of friends and is rest to the weary.

It is daylight to the discouraged, sunshine to the sad and nature's best evidence of love.

Imagine the power of a simple smile shown to another! We must be those who express the joy of the Lord. A number of years ago, the Lord really impressed upon me the importance of smiling. That week, as I occasionally do, I was leading worship for our local church. I decided that I would smile as I sang to give honor to the Lord. After service was over a good friend of mine came up to me laughing. As he kiddingly poked me in the sides, he said, "Ha, Ha, I know what happened." Not knowing at all what he was talking about I said, "What do you mean? What happened?" Again he poked me and said, "I know, Ha, Ha." "What do you mean?" I said, totally puzzled. Finally, he unlocked the joke. "I know that you made a mistake while you were leading worship." "I did?" I said quite alarmed. "Yes, and you know it too, I saw you smiling," my friend said. The joke was on him obviously, but also on me. I apparently needed this revelation of smiling much more than I had thought. It will be impossible for us to lead others to the Lord Jesus Christ if they perceive that their lives would be as miserable as we might suggest ours are! Being a Christian is certainly not a life free of problems; however, being a Christian does allow us to know the One who has the answer for every problem. Love and joy should flow out of us in the most difficult situation as well as during the most wonderful time of blessing. It is this kind of life that will cause non-Christians to marvel and to seek the One that we love.

John's whole epistle was consumed with the thought of loving others. This must be our foundation in winning others to the Lord.

2. Realize Jesus Is The Purpose Of Life

"Nor is there salvation in any other, for there is no other name under heaven given among men by which we must be saved." (Acts 4:12)

"The thief does not come except to steal, and to kill, and to destroy. I have come that they may have life, and that they may have it more abundantly. (John 10:10)

The whole purpose of witnessing is to give purpose to lives. It will never cease to amaze me how many Christians hold the greatest key to life that anyone could ever possess, yet they are unwilling to give it to others. Jesus is the only way that we can have true life. We must realize that Jesus is the purpose of life and that true fulfillment can only come through Him. When Jesus looked out at the multitudes, He was moved with compassion. Why? They were sheep without a shepherd. In other words, they were people with no guidance. Jesus is the purpose of life. May we as Christians begin to realize this truth and share with others that the eternal Creator has a purpose for every life He has created, and He longs to reveal it.

3. Go Fishing

And Then He said to them, "Follow Me, and I will make you fishers of men." (Matthew 4:19)

How do we go fishing? In First Corinthians 9:19-23, the Apostle Paul, who turned the world upside down by his witnessing, gave us a wonderful insight. We are to be all things to all men. This does not imply that we are to live a life of sin to try and influence others. It carries the thought that we are to relate to others on their ground of reference rather than our own. Jesus ate with sinners. What a wonderful way to relate to others, on their home base, and remove the starchiness that church can often have for others. There are many pure ways that this can be accomplished. For example, dinners, sporting events, shopping trips, camping trips, fishing, hunting, and many others. By building into others' lives, we may find that the Lord is building bridges into their hearts. We may even discover that He will use the unsaved to speak to our hearts!

OUR GOAL IS TO WIN THE LOST, NOT TO BE LIKE THEM. YET, OUR GOAL IS TO WIN THE LOST.

4. The "Good Samaritan" Approach

This is the easiest, yet most neglected approach to winning the lost. In the story of the Good Samaritan, in Luke 10:25-37, it is important that we understand the Scriptural context. This story is told in response to a question that was posed to Jesus. He was asked, "How can we inherit eternal life?" He responded by reminding them of the two greatest commandments, we are to love the Lord with everything that is within us and to love our neighbor as ourselves. The questioner replied: *"And who is my neighbor?"* The Lord directly answered his question with the story of the Good Samaritan. I believe that each detail of this story illustrates a spiritual point. We can learn God's method of responding to the lost and dying through the Good Samaritan. How sad it is that often the Church reverses roles and plays the part of the Priest or Levite in rejecting or ignoring the lost. Let's consider this story to better understand how we can have an affect (God's way) on those that are hurting on the wayside.

THE GOOD SAMARITAN

1. The Good Samaritan is moved with compassion

The very foundation of the "Good Samaritan" approach will always begin with a heart that is moved with compassion. We see this often in the life of Christ. In Mark 6:34, we read, "And Jesus came out, saw a great multitude and was moved with compassion for them, because they were like sheep not having a shepherd. So He began to teach them many things." Every Christian should understand that their compassion will determine their effectiveness. We will only be able to affect the multitudes as He did when we are moved with compassion as He was.

It is interesting to note what Jesus was addressing in the lives of the disciples. At the beginning of Mark, chapter 6, when the disciples were sent out to minister, they came back from this great "revival meeting" with a false concept. "Lord, look at all that *we* have done and what *we* have taught" (Mark 6:30). They had little regard for the people they were sent to minister to. This is so often the case in our lives. Their hearts were saying, "Lord look at *our* work, look at *our* power, look at *our* great wisdom." At that point in their lives, their own "spirituality" and reputations meant more to them than their ministry to the people. They should have cried out, "Oh Lord, You should have seen the eyes of the blind man when they were opened; how he was able to see his children for the first time. Lord, how the leper rejoiced to be able to take his little daughter into his arms for the first time." Instead the disciples, like we are so often, were turned inward and not outward.

Look at the events of the following verses, as our faithful Shepherd begins to shepherd His little flock (the disciples). In verse 31 of Mark 6, Jesus had told the disciples they would go to a deserted place and rest. In verse 34, He is moved with compassion. In verse 35 and 36, the disciples revealed their true heart, and Jesus, as the Gentle Shepherd always does, addressed the problem. The disciples said, "This is a deserted place, and already the hour is late. Send them away, that they may go into the surrounding country and villages and buy themselves bread; for they have nothing to eat."

What were they saying? "Lord, You promised a time to ourselves. Get rid of these people." What was His reply? "You give them something to eat." Remember, the disciples had just returned from casting out many demons, anointing with oil and healing the sick. They had the ability to feed them, yet they were more interested in their kingdom, in their power and in their comfort, than in the care and comfort of others. What did the gentle and tender Shepherd do? He simply commanded them to be seated, gave thanks, and distributed the bread of life. He reveals to us His heart of compassion. We will only affect the multitude when our heart's response is like the Lord's. If we find ourselves lacking His compassion, one way we can tap into the well spring is through intercessory prayer. A transforming love fills our hearts for those we've wept for while on our knees before our heavenly Father. May we experience Christ's love for the lost in such a way that nothing else in life matters - our reputation, our goals, our position - only the approval of our Heavenly King.

2. The Good Samaritan went to him and bandaged his wounds

We now see the neighborly Good Samaritan going to this man in need and bandaging his wounds. He was willing to forsake his way to cause another to live. One of the greatest problems in the Church today is those who have forgotten the message of Christ. What is His message? Christ lived His message through what He said and what He did. His love proved that people are more important than success, self-gratitude, or position. We can rationalize our responsibility to reach out to others away with many different excuses. Yet, if we are honest, in the end it all comes back to people. We must not focus on our own wounds, but concentrate on caring for others.

It is said of General Robert E. Lee that he was once speaking in highest terms to Confederate President Jefferson Davis about another officer. Astonished at this glowing testimony, another officer who had overheard said to him, "General, do you know that the man of whom you speak so highly to the President is one of your bitterest enemies and misses no opportunity to malign you?" "Yes," replied General Lee, "but the President asked my opinion of him; he did not ask for his opinion of me."

The Good Samaritan lives a life of laying down his reputation and life and replies to the question, "And who is my neighbor?" with the answer, "The one to whom I must go and bandage his wounds."

3. The Good Samaritan poured on oil and wine

The pouring on of oil and wine is the most wonderful experience that comes with the thought of the Good Samaritan. It is here that he has the opportunity to share the gospel in word to the man. We must understand that the oil and wine have very deep meaning in the Scripture. It speaks of the actual blood of Christ and the Cross. The Good Samaritan was now explaining the Cross and the blood of Christ to this man in need. The word *Gethsemane* is actually defined as "oil press." We know that Jesus Christ took the cup during the Passover and declared that the wine was a token of His shed blood for us. It is important to understand that applying the oil was not the first step in caring for the wounded man. Instead, we see the Samaritan reaching out with compassion, bandaging the wounds and finally pouring in the oil (which speaks of witnessing about the Cross).

Recently, I asked a congregation to consider what the topic of conversation would be if they could spend five minutes alone with any unsaved individual. Most of us would feel compelled to proclaim the gospel. Yet, if we were to read First Corinthians 13, we would see a different story. Paul tells us that love is to be the cornerstone of our walk. He goes on to tell us that love comes before faith. What must come before the oil and the wine can be applied? What must come before faith? " We love you! "

We must be careful that we don't seek to reach people for our own self-gratitude, but rather as an opportunity to express the love of Christ that comes bubbling forth from our hearts. One of the reasons we are not affecting the multitudes the way Christ did is because we are striving to bring them to salvation instead of loving them. Our method is backwards. We must, first and foremost, love others and gain their trust. Then we will have ample opportunity to pour on the wine and the oil.

4. The Good Samaritan set him upon his own animal

The Good Samaritan did not leave this stranger. In the words of James, the Samaritan does not say in his heart, "Depart in peace, be warmed and filled." (James 2:16). Instead, he forsook his own comfort and allowed the wounded man to ride comfortably while he walked beside him. Like the Good Shepherd who was willing to forsake His comfort with the Father in eternity past, the Good Samaritan is willing to give up his own way to help others find a way, which is the fulfillment of the second commandment.

It is interesting to note that as we pour out to those hurting around us as an expression of God's love, God will also reveal a deeper measure of Himself to us. We see this progression illustrated for us in the life of the Good Samaritan. The story begins as he is moved with compassion for the dying man. Our walk with God begins at salvation when we receive a measure of His compassion. He was then called to go and bandage the man's wounds, which we begin to receive soon after salvation, as God begins to place His call, His vision, and His healing touch upon us. He then is called to begin to share the gospel in a deeper measure, as we also can share the love of Christ with others, after experiencing it in a deeper fashion ourselves. He is now called upon to understand the cost of discipleship. It is very costly to win converts. Many converts have been won and lost due to lack of care. How the heart of God is looking for those "Samaritans" who would simply sacrifice their own "animals" (convenience) for the sake of others.

Consider what would or could come before you and others. Your house? Your car? Your job? Your family? Your ministry? We must be willing to forsake all to follow after Christ. The Good Samaritan was willing to forsake what mattered most to him. He was willing to reply, "My neighbor deserves my comfort."

5. The Good Samaritan brought him to the inn and took care of him

We must be willing to not only go the extra mile, but be willing to go the last mile. The Good Samaritan understood the importance of constant and continued care. After bringing the wounded man to the safety of the inn, he made provision for any needs that would arise. How many are in our inn that we are taking care of? Most of our inns have closed down due to lack of business. This Good Samaritan's inn was full to capacity with one man. Think on this for a moment: "Full to capacity with one man." We so often can look for the multitudes that we forget they are made up entirely of individuals. It has been said that if each person were to bring one other person to the Lord in one year, our churches would double. If each one of those people would then lead another to the Lord and each of those another, in two years our churches would then quadruple. If a church of 50 people would carry out this experiment over a five year period, it would then have 1,600 people!

In many cases, God does not choose to move in that way. On the other hand, He is looking for those who will be His hand extended to the needy. God desires that His Church would love the lost into the Kingdom and continue to love them into maturity. God is interested in preservation, not just birth. The Good Samaritan does not just bring his neighbor in but is also very concerned for his continued care and complete restoration of health.

As a side note, I would like to address one thought very quickly: God does want to fill our churches. Obviously, our vision is to see the multitudes come to Christ. We must not look at new members as another dollar added to the congregational coffers; but we must look at each new member as another life touched for the glory of God - another missionary sent out, another single mother helped, another orphan given food. God is interested in the multitudes, according to Second Peter 3:9. Does God desire that any should perish? No, absolutely none! We should be asking God to fill our churches not for ***our*** glory but for ***His*** glory.

6. The Good Samaritan left him in the care of others

After all the loving care the Good Samaritan provided, he was then called to move on. What if God calls us to a new geographical place, who will be responsible for the young converts God has given us? The Lord in His mercy does not leave us to wonder. We must carefully place each tender heart in the hands of another whom we trust and know will take care of this most precious cargo.

And who is your neighbor? The Good Samaritan tells us it is anyone in need. How far do we go in our witnessing, in helping the needy? The Good Samaritan instructs us again, ***to the end***.

5. A Practical Way to Witness Is to Build Tents

Acts 18:1-3 - *After these things Paul departed from Athens and went to Corinth. And he found a certain Jew named Aquila, born in Pontus, who had recently come from Italy with his wife Priscilla (because Claudius had commanded all the Jews to depart from Rome); and he came to them. So, because he was of the same trade, he stayed with them and worked; for by occupation they were tentmakers.*

Another good place to be an effective witness is our place of employment. However, we must be careful that we are not robbing our employer of time that rightfully belongs to him. There is nothing more dishonoring to God than an employee who is so interested in witnessing that he or she fails to get their job accomplished. On the other hand, we do not want to use this as an excuse to avoid witnessing, as there are proper and appropriate times we can share the Lord with others. Our fellow worker's eternal destiny can be dependent upon our attitudes, actions and words at our workplace. A good question that we must evaluate ourselves with at all times is "Do I really care enough about my fellow employee's eternal destination?"

6. We Must Pray for Others in Order to Be an Effective Witness

This is one area that has become insignificant in the minds of many Christians. The Apostles understood the power in prayer. We find in the book of Acts that they not only prayed for the salvation of souls, but also (and maybe more importantly), they prayed for boldness. It is further proof that we cannot be an effective witness until God has done a work in regard to our reputation. Our fear of what men think of us, must die. We can find in the life of Christ that He became one of no reputation. And in order for us to truly reveal Christ, we must be like Him in this respect.

Our prayers should be specific; Jesus always prayed very specifically. You can find Him praying for the simplest of items, in praying for thanks before they ate as well as the most important when He prayed for Peter's faith. Our prayer life, especially with the connection of how specifically we pray, will dictate how important a person's soul really is to us. How much are we found praying for others? Are their eternal souls really that important to us?

One last thought on this matter of prayer - do we pray for others in the Body of Christ? If we are truly concerned about the souls of others, then we will unite with the Body of Christ collectively. We don't want to be concerned about **our** churches flourishing and **our** membership growing. All that will matter is that souls are being rescued from darkness. We do not want to be carnal Christians concerned with carnal issues. We want to be men and women who are given to advancing the cause of Christ and His cause alone.

For when one says, "I am of Paul," and another, "I am of Apollos," are you not carnal? Who then is Paul, and who is Apollos, but ministers through whom you believed, as the Lord gave to each one? I planted, Apollos watered, but God gave the increase. So then neither he who plants is anything, nor he who waters, but God who gives the increase. (1 Corinthians 3:4-7)

7. To Be an Effective Witness, We Must Venture Outside of Israel

In other words, we must venture outside of our local churches to win the lost. The Church is wonderful, but the lost are not usually found there. Jesus was willing to eat with sinners, talk with sinners, and mingle with sinners. This was usually done in their homes or in their areas of reference, as we have previously noted. We must be careful not to come to the conclusion that God will always bring those who are hungry into our churches. This is not trusting in the sovereignty of God. God can speak many different ways and use many different methods to win others to Him. God cannot be confined to one certain pattern. We want to be willing to speak to anyone at anytime about anything when God is prompting us. Most often we will find ourselves in this position outside of the Church. We are not to be afraid, but, as the Scripture declares in the book of Proverbs, we are to be as bold as a lion, recognizing that we hold the deepest truth known to mankind.

Along with this thought, we should also feel a liberty to encourage those "inside of Israel." There is a time to suggest a change of scenery for those in other churches who are not growing. We are not to be afraid of being labeled a "sheep stealer." We are told in Scripture that Jesus' sheep will hear His voice. If a sheep is not hearing his Shepherd's voice, it is quite natural to seek a place where the voice of the Shepherd can be heard. If we sincerely feel the Holy Spirit is leading us, it is fine to recommend a change of scenery. However, this should not become a pattern in our lives.

NOTE: I want to make an important point here. We should *never* attack another leader. Leaders are appointed by God; therefore we are attacking God if we speak against them. Also, God has given the local pastor the grace for counsel over his sheep. Never violate this! It will produce one thing - error. Be very careful in this area of "venturing inside of Israel."

In closing this section on witnessing, I want to stress one thought. I have simply shared a few guidelines for witnessing and not rules. I am in no way suggesting that I have the step-by-step formula for success. Sharing the Lord with others is a very private, intense, and spiritual exercise that should be weighed with the highest of thought and discernment. I would hope that the most important truth we could possibly share with others is that we are concerned and caring people who have come to share a wonderful life with them. So much of witnessing has been pounding the Scripture - many times with right motives - in such a way that it has been very offensive. We are not called to "blow people away" with verses from the Bible. This is not what is found in the life of Christ, and I would oppose anyone who would suggest such a thing. Jesus is to be shared with the recognition and understanding that He is not willing that any should perish. With this understanding may we share Him with the love and compassion by which He came. May we begin, again, to truly love others!

THE GREATEST KEY TO WITNESSING IS TO LOVE PEOPLE

John is often referred to as the eagle, as we can understand by the four faces seen in Ezekial 1:6-10 (lion, ox, man and eagle). John's Gospel is the eagle that takes us into the heavenlies and allows us to see Jesus in the Spirit more than any other Gospel. Jesus is seen as the lion in Matthew, the ox in Mark, the man in Luke, and the eagle in John. Jesus also declared to His disciples, especially those who were fishermen, that they were to be fishers of men. John depicts an eagle fishing. He is the eagle who is found fishing for men. He is the spiritual eagle sharing with us the secrets of Heaven, and leading others according to the spirit rather than by preconceived ideas or methods of evangelism. John, the eagle, knew that his only hope was Christ Jesus, for without Him he could do nothing (John 15:5).

THE MESSAGE OF LOVE (PART IV)

1 JOHN 4:12-16

No one has seen God at any time. If we love one another, God abides in us, and His love has been perfected in us. By this we know that we abide in Him, and He in us, because He has given us of His Spirit. And we have seen and testify that the Father has sent the Son as Savior of the world. Whoever confesses that Jesus is the Son of God, God abides in him, and he in God. And we have known and believed the love that God has for us. God is love, and he who abides in love abides in God, and God in him.

In reading the epistle of John, the reader could easily come to the conclusion that John never speaks of anything but love. It seems that his emphasis goes no further. Yet, John, writing under the inspiration of the Lord, is taking us deeper. He is taking us on a journey where we can understand new truths along the way. He is revealing the divine nature of the man that he walked with for three and a half years. We will begin to see an unfolding picture of the precious relationship between the Son and His Father. He has given us a portrait of Heaven's love.

John now writes to us about a title. In the world today, titles have become a driving force in many lives. A man will abandon his friends, home, and sometimes even his family to obtain position as president of a company or a director of a business. Many men and women measure success by their titles. In God's Kingdom, titles have also been given. We read of priests, kings, prophets, pastors, evangelists and many others. Yet, we see a simple title that may carry the highest honor in Scripture. God is defined as the "God of Love." What a statement John makes! ***God is love***. In those three little words, John defines the infinite God. How can we write anything deeper? God is love. How can we possibly define that statement? It is so deep and so infinite that words are not able to define it further, yet it is so wonderful a truth that there is no definition needed. God is love. Those three words say it all! It explains the Cross. It explains the Creation of the world. It explains the Tribulation period, it explains why Jesus came to earth; it explains everything.

Yet, John ties this in with another thought. If we love God, we will abide in love. Why? Because that's what God is, that's what God is about. Remember, this is not John's fleshly conclusion; this is what he saw and what he heard. He must have remembered every miracle that Jesus had performed. Following is a list of just some of the acts of Christ found in the Gospel of John that would reveal the love of Jesus.

He changes water to wine	He witnesses to Nicodemus
He witnesses to the woman at the well	He heals the impotent man
He feeds the five thousand	He forgives the woman of adultery
He heals the blind man	He raises Lazarus from the dead
He washes the disciples' feet	He comforts the disciples
He prays for all believers	He hangs upon the cross

It is no wonder that John would write at the conclusion of his Gospel account that all of the books of the world could not contain what Jesus had done. How could you ever finish writing of One who **is** love? The book is still being written through the true disciples of Christ.

If we were to analyze your life by the statement, ______________________ is love. Would it be true of you? (Insert Your Name)

FEAR, JUDGMENT AND LOVE

1 JOHN 4:17-21

Love has been perfected among us in this: that we may have boldness in the day of judgment; because as He is, so are we in this world. There is no fear in love; but perfect love casts out fear, because fear involves torment. But he who fears has not been made perfect in love. We love Him because He first loved us. If someone says, "I love God," and hates his brother, he is a liar; for he who does not love his brother whom he has seen, how can he love God whom he has not seen? And this commandment we have from Him: that he who loves God must love his brother also.

Again, John is writing to us about the message of love. In these verses, however, he begins to tie in the message of love with the thought of fear. He writes to us that fear involves torment, yet love does not involve fear. John is making a distinction between those who live in love and those who live without the love of Christ. For those who are without Christ should and will live a life full of fear. There will be both eternal and natural judgment for those who have chosen not to live with the privilege of a love relationship with their God. However, if we are like Him and are striving to live with this relationship of love, we do not need to fear judgment from the One we love. Judgment can be a good word to the righteous. Let us look at one particular truth that John had seen and heard in the life of Christ. We find this truth in the words of Jesus to the Pharisees in John 8:38-45. It is one of the most direct, awesome statements ever spoken and recorded by man.

"I speak what I have seen with My Father, and you do what you have seen with your father." They answered and said to Him, "Abraham is our father." Jesus said to them, "If you were Abraham's children, you would do the works of Abraham. "But now you seek to kill Me, a Man who has told you the truth which I heard from God. Abraham did not do this. You do the deeds of

> *your father." Then they said to Him, "We were not born of fornication; we have one Father; God." Jesus said to them, "If God were your Father, you would love Me, for I proceeded forth and came from God; nor have I come of Myself, but He sent Me. Why do you not understand My speech? Because you are not able to listen to My word. You are of your father the devil, and the desires of your father you want to do. He was a murderer from the beginning, and does not stand in the truth, because there is no truth in him. When he speaks a lie, he speaks from his own resources, for he is a liar and the father of it. But because I tell the truth, you do not believe Me. (John 8:38-45)*

What a truth! Jesus says the Pharisees' father is the devil. Many would say that the loving Christ could not have spoken such harsh words. As the Prophet Isaiah would declare to us, "*to the law and to the testimony.*"In other words, let the Scripture speak! Let's analyze what Jesus was really saying. He began this discourse by saying to them, "I speak what I have seen with My Father, and you do what you have seen with your father." The defining sentence mentioned here declares to us that there are "two fathers." As we consider the contrast between the words of Christ and the words of the Pharisees we will gain a deeper understanding of these "two fathers."

The Pharisees thought they had a wonderful discourse and a wonderful argument, "Abraham is our father." They were trusting in their natural position and "old manna" (or the word of many years ago) rather than in the fresh revelation Jesus was trying to reveal to them. How sad it is to see the Pharisees' response. But how often are we guilty of the same? Whenever the Pharisees were confronted with truth, they were quick to discount the truth and point a finger at the flesh. Look at their response, "*We were not born of fornication.*" What were they saying? "Look at Your flesh, look at Your problems, look at Your inabilities." With one breath, they proclaimed their dedication to God above, and with the next breath they railed out accusations against ***His Son***. What an awesome and grave mistake they made. They were not rejecting the words of a man, they were rejecting the Word of God which had come in the flesh. That is why Jesus said their father was the devil. We are either partakers of life or death. There is no in-between. Every word that proceeds out of the mouth of a man will reveal life or death. This is what John is talking about: if we walk in love, we will walk with the God who is love, but on the other hand, if we walk with hatred, malice, or envy, our father is the devil, and we walk in fear because we are walking with the one whose very being intimates fear and torment. Perfect love casts away fear because the Father of love has conquered every power of the enemy on the Cross. John knew well the difference between the thought of fear and love. John knew well that this difference was indeed life and death, because this thought involved in totality the Kingdom of Satan and the Kingdom of God. These Kingdoms cannot and will not coexist; the real question that John is asking us is, "To which Kingdom do you belong?"

> *You cannot drink the cup of the Lord and the cup of demons too; you cannot have a part in both the Lord's table and the table of demons.*(1 Corinthians 10:21)

Chapter 6

HOW DO WE OVERCOME THE WORLD?

FIRST JOHN FIVE

The First Step to Overcoming the World

1 John 5:1-6

Whoever believes that Jesus is the Christ is born of God, and everyone who loves Him who begot also loves him who is begotten of Him. By this we know that we love the children of God, when we love God and keep His commandments. For this is the love of God, that we keep His commandments. And His commandments are not burdensome. For whatever is born of God overcomes the world. And this is the victory that has overcome the world; our faith. Who is he who overcomes the world, but he who believes that Jesus is the Son of God? This is He who came by water and blood; Jesus Christ; not only by water, but by water and blood. And it is the Spirit who bears witness, because the Spirit is truth.

John now answers the age-old question that tugs on the heart strings of every Christian who is truly seeking to be like the Lord. How do we overcome the world? As we confess that Jesus is our Lord, we are declaring (before Heaven and Earth) that He will be our King, and He will rule and reign over the kingdoms of our heart. At salvation, we are simply joining all of God's majestic creation in the declaration of His Kingship. As we look closely at this portion of First John, we will see that John is presenting the precious truth of living a victorious life and providing us with the key to victory. It seems as though he just slipped in a little statement, *this is He who came by water and blood; Jesus Christ; not only by water, but by water and blood.* Now why would he have told us this little fact after declaring to us that we are to overcome the world through faith? We must remember that John is writing to us about what he had seen and heard. It is foundationally necessary to keep that one little fact in our minds in order to understand his epistle. So......what had John seen and heard?

But when they came to Jesus, and saw that He was dead already, they brake not His legs: But one of the soldiers with a spear pierced His side, and forthwith came there out blood and water. (John 19:33,34)

The Gospel of John is the only Gospel that mentions that at the scene of the cross, blood and water came out. Is this just a mere coincidence that in his epistle he mentions that Christ the Overcomer is synonymous with the water and blood. What is he trying to tell us? It might seem to some that there is a contradiction of thought here. Wasn't John writing about overcoming by faith, and yet now he is writing to us about the Cross? Aren't these two different doctrinal thoughts? Let's consider just how much these two thoughts were interwoven in the life of Jesus on a daily basis.

The book of Isaiah gives us an interesting picture of the daily relationship of the Lord Jesus Christ and His Heavenly Father. We read, *"The Lord God has given Me the tongue of the learned, That I should know how to speak a word in season to him who is weary. He awakens Me morning by morning, He awakens My ear to hear as the learned. The Lord GOD has opened My ear; And I was not rebellious, nor did I turn away. I gave My back to those who struck Me, and My cheeks to those who plucked out the beard; I did not hide My face from shame and spitting* (Isaiah 50:4-6). We find out that every morning the Lord was awakened by the Father with the message of the Cross. Was this only in a futuristic sense? Was He only hearing about what would happen in the years to come? Remember that the Lord Himself told us that we are to take up our cross daily. Wouldn't it be safe to assume that He also was found taking up His cross or laying down His own desires? Let's look at a few examples in the life of Christ to see how He lived the message of the Cross. If we're willing to follow in His footsteps, we too, can overcome the world.

> *The two disciples heard Him speak, and they followed Jesus. Then Jesus turned, and seeing them following, said to them, "What do you seek?" They said to Him, "Rabbi (which is to say, when translated, Teacher), where are You staying?" He said to them, "Come and see." They came and saw where He was staying, and*

remained with Him that day (now it was about the tenth hour). (John 1:37-39)

What do we see here? For thirty years Jesus enjoyed a fairly secluded life. He must have spent countless hours in the presence of His Father without interruption. He must have loved and longed for the precious times of communing with His Father. Suddenly one day, His ear was awakened. "What is that You're saying to me, Father?" What did the Father reveal to the Son? What did the Father whisper into the ear of the Son? "Son, today You will have to embrace the loss of privacy, today Your cross is the cross of self-denial." Of course we know there was only one way the Son would respond, with total obedience. But from that day forward, Jesus no longer had privacy. He would be surrounded by His disciples, the multitudes and religious leaders. Yet, when the cross of self-denial and His loss of privacy was presented to Him, He responded with a simple "Yes" to the Father.

On the third day there was a wedding in Cana of Galilee, and the mother of Jesus was there. Now both Jesus and His disciples were invited to the wedding. And when they ran out of wine, the mother of Jesus said to Him, "They have no wine." Jesus said to her, "Woman, what does your concern have to do with Me? My hour has not yet come." His mother said to the servants, "Whatever He says to you, do it." Now there were set there six waterpots of stone, according to the manner of purification of the Jews, containing twenty or thirty gallons apiece. Jesus said to them, "Fill the waterpots with water." And they filled them up to the brim. And He said to them, "Draw some out now, and take it to the master of the feast." And they took it. When the master of the feast had tasted the water that was made wine, and did not know where it came from (but the servants who had drawn the water knew), the master of the feast called the bridegroom. (John 2:1-9)

If we were to visit the scene before the scene, what do you think we would see? Jesus must have been enjoying wonderful fellowship with His disciples. He must have longed for opportunities like this one to share with them the deep truths of the Kingdom of Heaven. The anointing and approval of Heaven was upon every word that He spoke. As He was pouring out His heart, He was interrupted once again by the voice of the Father. "Son, today You must be willing to give up Your right to fellowship. There is a greater need." The cross of surrendering His desire for fellowship and serving others was presented, and once again we see Him responding in total obedience and replying "Yes" to the Father. The cross was not an experience for Jesus merely at the end of His life. **Everyday** His ear was awakened with the words of the cross. Let's consider one last example to gain further understanding how every detail of His life was consumed with the message of the cross.

Now the Passover of the Jews was at hand, and Jesus went up to Jerusalem. And He found in the temple those who sold oxen and sheep and doves, and the moneychangers doing business. When He had made a whip of cords, He drove them all out of the temple, with the sheep and the oxen, and poured out the changers' money and overturned the tables. And He said to those who sold doves, "Take these things away! Do not make My Father's house a house of merchandise!" Then His disciples remembered that it was written, "Zeal for Your house has eaten Me up." So the Jews answered and said to Him, "What sign do You show to us, since You do these things?" Jesus answered and said to them, "Destroy this temple, and in three days I will raise it up." (John 2:13-19)

In this scene, many must have assumed He was wrong in what He was doing. Imagine what the disciples must have thought. "Wait a minute, I thought we were to love our enemies?" or "Wait, how can this be? Aren't we supposed to be peacemakers?" It must have seemed so inconsistent. The cross always will. It must have seemed very foolish for this 33 1/2 year old man to die upon a cross, and even more foolish for Him to embrace it every day of His life. It is only when we lose our own reputation as Jesus did, that we can find the exaltation that only the cross can bring. On that day the Father once again came to the Son. "Son, are You ready to lose your reputation? Are You ready for others to think that Your walk with Me is foolish? Are You ready for others to think that You are a crazy man?" Once again Jesus would embrace the cross that the Father asked Him to carry. He understood that He would lose His reputation and carry reproach. Yet, we see His resolution and love for the Father as He bowed before the throne and responded "Yes" to the Father.

We can look at these examples and become easily discouraged. Is that all that I have to look forward to - a life of denial? But consider the end result! By embracing the loss of privacy, He was privileged to walk with disciples that became mighty men of God. By embracing the loss of fellowship, the Lord was allowed to turn water into wine. By embracing His loss of reputation, He was able to prophesy about the days to come. What a wonderful privilege! The cross will always bring tremendous life. If we will simply give our lives, in faith to God, then He will overcome the world in us through the *power of the cross.*

> *Therefore if there is any consolation in Christ, if any comfort of love, if any fellowship of the Spirit, if any affection and mercy, fulfill my joy by being like-minded, having the same love, being of one accord, of one mind. Let nothing be done through selfish ambition or conceit, but in lowliness of mind let each esteem others better than himself. Let each of you look out not only for his own interests, but also for the interests of others. Let this mind be in you which was also in Christ Jesus, who, being in the form of God, did not consider it robbery to be equal with God, but made Himself of no reputation, taking the form of a bondservant, and coming in the likeness of men. And being found in appearance as a man, He humbled Himself and became obedient to the point of death, even the death of the cross. Therefore God also has highly exalted Him and given Him the name which is above every name, that at the name of Jesus every knee should bow, of those in heaven, and of those on earth, and of those under the earth, and that every tongue should confess that Jesus Christ is Lord, to the glory of God the Father. (Philippians 2:1-11)*

During one of my devotional times with the Lord, I was smitten with a thought that shook many of my foundational thoughts. I was reading a verse that we have all read many times and most likely heard preached in a number of different ways; "Not my will, but thine be done." I began to think of the decisions I had made for the Lord during my life and how utterly ridiculous they must have seemed to others. As a very young Christian I had a very successful job in a large corporation. One day one of the executives for that company came and offered me an excellent promotion. I would be transferred to another city and would become the supervisor of a very large department and receive quite an increase in pay. In the natural, I would have jumped at this wonderful opportunity. But I had a problem, the Lord had spoken to me a few months before that I was to stay at the church I was attending for a length of time which was not yet completed. I could have reasoned this decision away and taken the promotion, but I knew that would not be pleasing to the Lord, so with much anxiety I turned the promotion down. The company was so offended by my decision, that they actually demoted me. Imagine, what others must have thought. He really missed the boat. He must have received too many hard hits while he played hockey; what a bad decision. However, in the eyes of others, my string of bad decisions was just beginning. A number of years later, the Lord spoke to me to go into the construction business. Now to others, this might not sound too foolish, but I had absolutely no experience, an excellent job at the time and a baby on the way. In obedience, to God's voice, I went into this business. Four months later, my family had no food, no money for rent, no wonderful testimonies, and I was making approximately $1.50 to $3.00 per hour. What a testimony! I couldn't wait to tell my parents about the blessing of the Lord, yet I (and probably only my wife and I) knew the Lord was in it. Unexpectedly, I was offered a wonderful promotion. I became the manager of a construction company. Although my first year there was difficult, God seemed to bless the second year, and I was enjoying (actually loving) my job. Suddenly it happened again (yes, you guessed it), God spoke. "Sell everything that you have and go to Bible school." I did not want to go to Bible school, I enjoyed the comfort of my home, friends and church, yet in obedience we went to Bible school. Imagine again, what others must have thought. What is he doing? Does this man have any sense? After completing two years of Bible school a very curious thing happened. A few weeks before graduation, I was called and told that due to circumstances I would not be able to graduate with my class but would receive my diploma at home. Can you imagine the following discussion:

Kirk: Well, Dad, I'm home from Bible school.
Dad: Welcome home!" my Dad replied. "Well did you get good grades?
Kirk: I sure did. I received all A's.
Dad: Wow, could I take a look at your diploma?
Kirk: Oh (with a very long pause), I didn't get one.
Dad: What? You didn't get a diploma, what happened?
Kirk: Well (with a longer pause), they didn't think I deserved one; but don't worry Dad, I've been offered a position already with a church.
Dad: Excellent, I bet they are going to give you a good salary.
Kirk: Well (another long pause, followed by a very quick sentence) about $100.00 a week.
Dad: $100.00 per week? You can't live on that! Oh, but they must be providing you with a wonderful house since you have such a large family.
Kirk: Well (with the longest pause), it does have *one* bedroom.

Imagine what my father and others must have thought. This man does not know how to do anything right. Yet, we knew we were walking this simple life of obedience to God's voice. A few short years later, the Lord opened a door to a business proposition that involved nearly a million dollars in construction work. My business partner and I did this work and made a tremendous amount of profit. Finally, I would look successful, finally others would say that I had made it. However, (you guessed it), again the Lord spoke, "Give all of your money to the Kingdom, to the work of the Lord." In obedience, we gave away the profit of this business. In obedience, we once again looked foolish. As I pondered this short story of my life, I began to realize that we had followed after the will of the Lord. We had given up much for His way and His life. Then the Lord spoke some words that shook me that day and hopefully will shake you. "What you did yesterday is not important, *what are you doing today?*' It is so easy for us to begin to provide the Lord with our list of past accomplishments and sacrifices, yet what is important to Him is what we are doing today. The Lordship of Christ in our lives has as much to do with today than with any other day. Jesus could have walked wonderfully upon the earth for 3 1/2 years, and yet if the final act of the cross was not carried out in obedience, it would have all been in vain. We must evaluate our lives constantly and ask ourselves honestly, "Lord Jesus, is Your will being accomplished in my life, for it is not my will but Thine be done." Are you embracing the cross of Christ for your life? Does He awaken you morning by morning to the sound of His voice, and when He does, how do you respond?

Testimony of the Son

1 John 5:6-13

This is He who came by water and blood; Jesus Christ; not only by water, but by water and blood. And it is the Spirit who bears witness, because the Spirit is truth. For there are three that bear witness in heaven: the Father, the Word, and the Holy Spirit; and these three are one. And there are three that bear witness on earth: the Spirit, the water, and the blood; and these three agree as one. If we receive the witness of men, the witness of God is greater; for this is the witness of God which He has testified of His Son. He who believes in the Son of God has the witness in himself; he who does not believe God has made Him a liar, because he has not believed the testimony that God has given of His Son. And this is the testimony: that God has given us eternal life, and this life is in His Son. He who has the Son has life; he who does not have the Son of God does not have life. These things I have written to you who believe in the name of the Son of God, that you may know that you have eternal life, and that you may continue to believe in the name of the Son of God.

John writes to us in verse 12, "He who has the Son has life; he who does not have the Son of God does not have life." John is making a very clear doctrinal statement here that we all understand and, as Christians, must be in agreement with. What was it that John heard and saw that would have made him make this statement? Since we are living in an hour in which many churches relegate this statement that there is only life in Christ to legalism or a narrow-minded approach to Christianity, we must ask, "What would Jesus tell us?" And in a deeper sense, what **did** He tell us? Let's examine the words of John and the truths presented in John 5:31-47.

> *"If I bear witness of Myself, My witness is not true. There is another who bears witness of Me, and I know that the witness which He witnesses of Me is true. You have sent to John, and he has borne witness to the truth. Yet I do not receive testimony from man, but I say these things that you may be saved. He was the burning and shining lamp, and you were willing for a time to rejoice in his light. (John 5:31-35)*

Many Christians are motivated (or driven) by the pursuit of success. They desire to be successful in the eyes of man by accomplishing great things for God. However, if we seek to testify of the Son, we will not be striving for our own testimony, and we will certainly not be testifying of ourselves. Even in these few verses He is not found expounding on and lifting up His own ministry; rather He elevates the ministry of another, the ministry of John the Baptist. He was not looking for a large name or a huge following. In the Kingdom of Heaven we are guaranteed that if we exalt ourselves, we will be abased. Jesus was willing to walk His life on this earth being abased so that throughout all of eternity He might be the exalted King of Kings. This is His testimony. By God's grace, may it be ours also!

> *"But I have a greater witness than John's; for the works which the Father has given Me to finish; the very works that I do; bear witness of Me, that the Father has sent*

Me. And the Father Himself, who sent Me, has testified of Me. You have neither heard His voice at any time, nor seen His form. But you do not have His word abiding in you, because whom He sent, Him you do not believe. (John 5:36-38)

If we are to have the testimony of the Son, we will have fruit. Jesus is found saying that His works bear witness of Him. We must also show some fruit in our lives that prove we are Christ's. Jesus, the source of life, will always bring forth life in every believer. We are not to judge our lives by the **amount** of the fruit, only by the fact that we bring forth **some** fruit. **Any fruit is fruit.** His testimony is life because He is life.

"You search the Scriptures, for in them you think you have eternal life; and these are they which testify of Me. But you are not willing to come to Me that you may have life. (John 5:39-40)

Jesus is clearly defining His testimony (for us). He is a God of relationship, as we have previously seen. He began by creating Adam and Eve for relationship, and He has never altered that plan or desire.

Jesus is our goal, not the Scriptures. Many years ago I asked the Lord how I could know the difference between truth and error. God spoke to me so clearly, that I can remember it as if it were yesterday. He said, "Any doctrine that attacks relationship is error." This thought has protected me from many false doctrines and other elements of error. We are not to look at the Scripture alone as our relationship. Only Christ can be our relationship. The thought that we can live our lives according to the principles of Scripture alone is not Scriptural. Jesus said, "I am the way, the truth, and the life" (John 14:6). All questions about the cornerstone of our faith and life should be answered by Scripture. However, there is no life apart from a relationship with Him. The testimony of the Son and those who walk with Him will always be centered around a true relationship with Him.

> *"I do not receive honor from men. But I know you, that you do not have the love of God in you. I have come in My Father's name, and you do not receive Me; if another comes in his own name, him you will receive. How can you believe, who receive honor from one another, and do not seek the honor that comes from the only God? (John 5:41-44)*

The Son does not seek to receive honor from men. In contrast, consider Saul for a moment. Saul's greatest weakness was his desire for man's approval. He begged Samuel to bless him in the eyes of the people and considered their approval to mean more than the approval of God. I want to point out one of the most awesome portions of Scripture in regard to God giving someone the desire of their heart. Saul wanted to be lifted up before men. What happened at his death? After losing his position as king (by his death), Saul's head was removed (he was not under authority, so his head was removed), and his body was hung upon the wall for all to see. He was literally lifted up for all men to see! Saul was given his desire, but how wrong it was!

Solomon cried out that the pleasures of this world are all vanity. May this truth be indelibly written upon the tablets of our hearts. What does it matter if we gain the approval and applause of men for seventy or eighty short years of life, if for eternity we regret the way we lived our lives? As we learn the ways of our Father, we will begin to make choices based upon what is pleasing to Him, and when we get to heaven, our life's fulfillment will be found in the words, "Well done, good and faithful servant." May God stamp eternity on our hearts and before our eyes, and may His blessing be our greatest asset.

> *"Do not think that I shall accuse you to the Father; there is one who accuses you; Moses, in whom you trust. For if you believed Moses, you would believe Me; for he wrote about Me. But if you do not believe his writings, how will you believe My words?" (John 5:45-47)*

The testimony of the Son brings out one of the most terrifying and amazing parts of the Bible that we can read. He declares that He will not accuse the Pharisees. Remember, this is the Son of God, the judge of all of the earth. He says Moses will accuse them. What did He mean by that? How could this be? We are not under the law. Jesus is saying that we will be judged by what we say we believe. Remember how the Pharisees said, "We have Moses and the law?" Imagine how the scene will be played in heaven. As the Pharisees present themselves before the judgment seat of Christ, their lives will be relived before all the host of heaven. Imagine the scene. "Father, let's play back their lives." What humiliation they will suffer as they watch themselves rejecting their Messiah and turning others away. But Jesus will turn to the Father and say, "No, Father, we will not condemn for that, because I said that I would not accuse them." The next scene will begin with Jesus' trial before the Pharisees as they loudly cry, "Let's kill Him!" And then again, before Pilate, they chant, "Crucify Him!" And again the scene will return to the Lamb seated upon the throne, "Father, My blood could have provided forgiveness, yet these men have declared they are under the Law of Moses." The court will then demand a reading of the Law of

Moses and for all of eternity these words will be heard by the Pharisees. "This law states that the punishment for killing (murder) is death." **By their own words, the Pharisees will be condemned forever.**

The words we speak carry tremendous power; we will be held accountable for every idle word we speak. If we are to carry the testimony of Christ, we must realize our complete inadequacy. He must reveal to us that we need Him in every aspect of our lives. In every situation, we need to speak His words and live His message. It is a sad truth that the Pharisees are in hell today not having learned this lesson when they were with Him. May we as Christians learn today to allow Him to control our tongues and our idle words. We *must* cry out for mercy as never before that we might have the testimony of the Son.

"He who has the Son has life; he who does not have the Son of God does not have life.

Prayer and Concern for the Brethren

1 John 5:14-21

Now this is the confidence that we have in Him, that if we ask anything according to His will, He hears us. And if we know that He hears us, whatever we ask, we know that we have the petitions that we have asked of Him. If anyone sees his brother sinning a sin which does not lead to death, he will ask, and He will give him life for those who commit sin not leading to death. There is sin leading to death. I do not say that he should pray about that. All unrighteousness is sin, and there is sin not leading to death. We know that whoever is born of God does not sin; but he who has been born of God keeps himself, and the wicked one does not touch him. We know that we are of God, and the whole world lies under the sway of the wicked one. And we know that the Son of God has come and has given us an understanding, that we may know Him who is true; and we are in Him who is true, in His Son Jesus Christ. This is the true God and eternal life. Little children, keep yourselves from idols. Amen.

John concludes this wonderful epistle by leading us back to prayer and concern for our brethren. The prayers of Jesus must have been indelibly marked in his memory. He remembered the countless hours Jesus spent interceding for the lives of others. The heart and mind of John in turn, was consumed with a love for the brethren. Some years ago, there was dissension between two women in our church. We began to pray that the Lord would solve this issue. He answered our prayers through a dream that caused me to understand the reason for their problem and the solution. In this dream, one woman was giving bread to the other. As fast as she gave the bread, she received new bread from the Lord. After some time, however, she began to withhold some of the bread, and as she withheld, so did God. Soon she was giving no bread and receiving no bread. I knew what the Lord was saying. She had hindered the flow of God's grace when she stopped pouring out to the other woman. I then encouraged her to begin the process of giving once again. As her heart reached out with love, the problems seemed to fade away. Why? One man stated it this way so well and so accurately, "We only have grace to do the will of God." We cannot stand without grace, and we cannot receive mercy without showing mercy.

A man or woman of God who wants to move closer to God must be constantly bringing others to Christ through a love relationship; and the only way to a love relationship with God is through many love relationships here. Our true love for the brethren will be proven by our level of concern for them. Do we carry their burdens in prayer or are we too concerned with our own prayer life? Are we giving out our bread or are we withholding what God has given? John knew what he had seen and heard in those wondrous years that he partook of his Saviour, John heard and saw love defined.

CONCLUSION

Let's imagine a grizzled old man quietly walking along the seashore oblivious to the crowds around him. In the distance the sun begins to rise over the small mountains that surround the sea. There are many others on the seashore this day. Most will pass the old man with little thought, others will pass him with contempt; still others, with a quiet respect and awe. The old man's eyes were not, however, on any of these people. He doesn't seem to notice the parade of prestigious and pompous men that are passing by. As he walks along, with his faithful staff in hand, his eyes have not lost their vision for what he has seen ahead. There in the distance was the group he had been watching and is walking toward. Who is this group? It is still a speck on the seashore for many; most would not even notice these people. But for the old man, he had an important appointment with them. As he gets closer, they suddenly come into view. But wait, this can't be who the old man had walked these many miles to see. This can't be the important meeting he had come for and spoken of. There are no people of honor here. Why did he come for these?

These are just children. Insignificant little children. But he begins to tell them a story. The old man begins slowly, yet with a burning love that is evident in his voice and in his life, "There once was a group of men, they were men of little understanding, but their hearts burned to do what was right. In this group, Children, was a man named Jesus. Jesus was the teacher of these men. He was a man that was holy and always did what was right. He came down from Heaven to die for us, so that through His death we might receive life. This man Jesus once illustrated to these men how important little children were to Him. They had been arguing, you see, about who was the most important, the most powerful. Jesus, who was a wonderful storyteller, would illustrate His story, with a little child, much like any of you. He once told them that being a great leader is not important, and then in the middle of His story, He sat a little child in the center of His disciples. Why do you think He did that? Why did He put this little child in the midst of them? He wanted to show them, Children, how important it was to love little ones. The ones who are not significant. A position, Jesus told them, was not the important thing. He had already told them the most important thing and would tell them again in a different way. He said, "You shall love the Lord your God with all your heart, with all your soul, and with all your mind. This is the first and great commandment. And the second is like it: "You shall love your neighbor as yourself" (Matthew 22:37-39). The old man then concluded his story and slowly forced himself off of the ground. "I must be going now, Children, but I promise I will come again." One of the children cried out, "But when, when will you come again?" The old man turned with determination and resolve and answered, "God willing, I will come often, Children, to visit you." And again from the group of children a question arose, "Sir, what is your name, you haven't told us your name, what is it?" The grizzled old man who had seen years of trouble and yet continued to love; the grizzled old man who had been scorned, rejected, and berated by men and yet continued to love, then turned and looked the small child in the eyes and began to cry. "My name, little one, you want to know my name? My name is the Church of the living God, for those who have ears to hear let them hear."

The epistle of John is not to be the story of John. It is to become the heart, the life and experience of every Christian. As we have read of this "*man called John*," will you allow the Scripture and God's voice to begin to burn within your life? And more importantly, will you once again allow your life to be consumed with a love for your God? The most awesome and terrifying thought the human mind can ponder must certainly be centered on our shortness of time. We live in an hour that many Christians believe is the end of time. However, whether this is true or not does not negate that our time on earth is extremely short. At the best, we have seventy or eighty years to cultivate a love relationship with our God. We do not have a moment to lose or a second to waste! John was first and foremost a lover of God, are you?

Other Books Available From Hebron Press

The Final Victory: The Year 2000

By Marvin Byers

This book is a bestseller and required reading in one of America's most respected and best known theological seminaries, yet many Christian bookstores are afraid to sell it! This book shares what the early Church and others, like Isaac Newton, declared about the end times. It shows how the Scriptures and events in the Middle East confirm their understanding. Decide for yourself after considering the compelling facts outlined in this incredible book!

TPB-336p. ISBN 1-56043-824-X (6" x 9" Paperback) Retail $12.99

Six Days and a Day

The Creator's Blueprint to Make Us Like Jesus

By Marvin Byers

The Creation account in Genesis, like every other miracle of Christ in the Bible, is full of truth and reveals God's ways and nature. Only the Creator could make a glorious new creation out of absolutely nothing. He wants to do the same in your life, making you into a new creation in Christ that is filled with the glory of the last Adam – the Lord Himself!

TPB-240p. ISBN 1-56043-263-2 (6" x 9" Paperback) Retail $12.99

Yasser Arafat - An Apocalyptic Character?

An Urgent Call to the Nation of Israel and the Body of Christ

By Marvin Byers

Daniel gives us approximately 80 prophetic details to help us identify a significant apocalyptic character when he comes. Yasser Arafat has fulfilled nearly 50 of these and is poised to fulfill the others very soon. Yet for the most part, the Church ignores him! Could this man actually be part of the fulfillment of God's end time prophetic message?

TPB-262p. ISBN 0-9647871-3-X (6" x 9" Paperback) Retail $12.99

To Order – Send the retail cost above, plus *$2.50* shipping & handling to:

HEBRON MINISTRIES

2203 E. 11-Mile Rd., Royal Oak, MI 48067

For VISA or MasterCard orders ***Call 1-800-LAST-DAY (527-8329)***

HEBRON MINISTRIES

Do You Long for a Deeper Walk with The Lord?

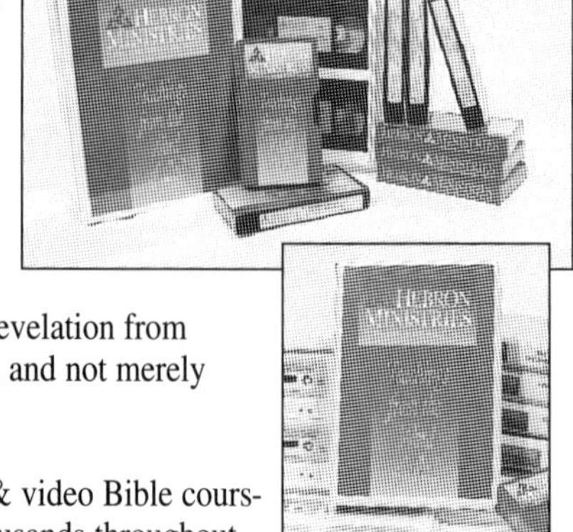

Hebron Ministries Audio & Video Tape In-depth Bible Courses

Does your heart long to know the Lord in a more meaningful and intimate way? The calling and ministry of ***Hebron Ministries*** is to share vital keys from God's Word that help hungry hearts experience the joy of His presence. Hebron's vision is to share revelation from God's Word that ministers to the heart, and not merely imparts academic information.

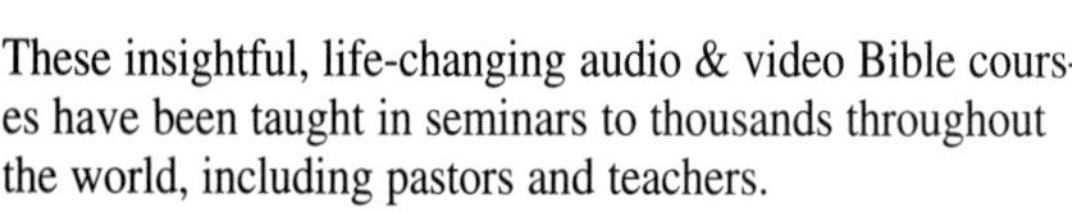

These insightful, life-changing audio & video Bible courses have been taught in seminars to thousands throughout the world, including pastors and teachers.

Courses Currently Available:

- **The Life of Christ (Parts 1-3)***
- **The Tabernacle of David and Worship**
- **Genesis (Parts 1-3)***
- **Foundations of the Faith (Parts 1-4)****
- **1,2 & 3 John**
- **Marriage and the Family (Parts 1-3)***
- **Divine Guidance and Counsel**
- **Revelation and Daniel (Parts 1-4)****
- **The Little Horn of Daniel**
- **The Millennium**

* 36 hour course **48 hour course

Many courses are also available in Spanish

Cost per 12 hours of teaching:

$59.95 Video $39.95 Audio

For VISA or MasterCard Orders call 1-800-LAST DAY (527-8329)